Mapping

THE Organizational

Psyche

Mapping
THE Organizational
Psyche

A JUNGIAN THEORY
OF ORGANIZATIONAL DYNAMICS
AND CHANGE

JOHN G. CORLETT
CAROL S. PEARSON

Center for Applications of Psychological Type, Inc. CAPT Gainesville, Florida

Published by
Center for Applications of Psychological Type, Inc.
2815 NW 13th Street, Suite 401
Gainesville, FL 32609
(352) 375-0160

CAPT™, the CAPT logo, and Center for Applications of Psychological Type™ are trademarks of the Center for Applications of Psychological Type, Inc., Gainesville, FL.

Myers-Briggs Type Indicator®, Myers-Briggs®, and MBTI® are trademarks or registered trademarks of the Myers-Briggs Type Indicator Trust in the United States and other countries.

The Organizational and Team Culture Indicator™ and the OTCI™ are trademarks or registered trademarks of CAPT in the United States and other countries.

The Pearson-Marr Archetype Indicator™ and the PMAI™ are trademarks or registered trademarks of CAPT in the United States and other countries.

The System Stewardship Survey™ is a trademark of John G. Corlett.

The Archetypal Leadership Styles Survey™ and the Archetypes of Family Culture™ are trademarks of Carol S. Pearson.

Printed in the United States of America.

Library of Congress Cataloging-in-Publication Data
Corlett, John G., 1948-
Mapping the organizational psyche : a Jungian theory of organizational dynamics
    and change / John G. Corlett and Carol S. Pearson.
p. cm.
Includes bibliographical references and index.
ISBN 0-935652-69-8
1. Organizational behavior. 2. Corporate culture. 3. Industrial management—
    Psychological aspects. 4. Corporations—Public relations—Psychological
    aspects. 5. Psychology, Industrial. 6. Psychological, Applied. 7. Jungian
    psychology. I. Pearson, Carol, 1944- II. Title.

HD58.7.C636 2003
158.7—dc21

                                                                    2003043988

To Ellie, my soul's mate.

—JOHN G. CORLETT

To my wonderful son, Jeffrey.

—CAROL S. PEARSON

CON | TENTS

Acknowledgments *ix*

Introduction *xi*

Prologue **1**

PART ONE: Surveying the Organizational Psyche

Chapter One
The Organizational Psyche: An Overview **7**

Chapter Two
The Organizational Psyche: The Unconscious Realm **13**

Chapter Three
The Organizational Psyche: The Conscious Realm **27**

Chapter Four
Organizational Psychodynamics: Pitfalls **37**

Chapter Five
Organizational Psychodynamics: Pathways **53**

Chapter Six
Getting Down to Cases **69**

Chapter Seven
Creating Wholeness: Leading the Organizational Psyche **85**

Chapter Eight
Restoring Wholeness: Consulting to the Organizational Psyche **99**

Chapter Nine
Hermetic Transformation **107**

PART TWO: Plotting Your Organization's Psyche

Task One
Your Organization's Psyche: What's There and What's Working? **117**

Task Two
Your Organization's Psyche: What's Not Working? **125**

Task Three
Your Organization's Psyche: Moving Toward Wholeness **129**

Task Four
Pulling it All Together **133**

Task Five
   Plotting a Leader's Psyche **137**
Task Six
   Plotting a Consultant's Psyche **149**

Appendices
Appendix A: MBTI® Type Descriptions **159**
Appendix B: System Stewardship Survey™ **163**
Appendix C: Archetypal Leadership Styles Survey™ **169**
Appendix D: Archetypes of Family Cultures™ **179**

Glossary 183

Resources 189

References 191

Index 199

About the Authors 205

ACKNOWLEDG | MENTS

I am deeply grateful to Jim and Annette Cullipher, creators and sustainers of the Journey into Wholeness, Inc., for providing me with a true *temenos*— a place where over the past dozen years much of my learning about Jungian concepts has taken place.

Thanks to Patricia, Kathleen, and the rest of our self-managed gang for co-creating with me an action learning laboratory where we all learned about systems, consultant congruence, the shadow, and integrity.

I am most appreciative of Don Klein and the other members of my Union Institute doctoral dissertation committee for stoking the academic fires in which many of the ideas I have contributed to this book were initially tempered.

My appreciation goes, as well, to Carol S. Pearson and the special professional and intellectual partnership with her that goes back more than seven years. It took root in conversations stemming from Carol's reading of my doctoral dissertation. It sprouted tender shoots in the course of many conversations; it put out sturdy branches in two workshops we led together; and it blossomed in the writing of this book, as we discovered the energy in the creative tension between our respective points of view.

And thanks from the deepest places in me to my wife, Eleanor, for her ongoing mentorship around things of the heart and for her abiding trust in and support of this project.

— JOHN G. CORLETT

I am grateful to Elizabeth Styron, president of the Center for Applications of Psychological Type (CAPT) and Eleanor K. Sommer, editorial director at CAPT for their commitment to publishing and promoting my work applying Jungian psychology to human, leadership, and organizational development. I also so appreciate Eleanor's careful and able editing of the manuscript. *Mapping the Organizational Psyche* is part of a larger CAPT project that includes instrumentation (such as the *Pearson-Marr Archetype Indicator*™ and the *Organizational and Team Culture Indicator*™ instruments), professional training programs, and various supporting materials. This book provides a theoretical background to support the informed organizational use of applied Jungian concepts—including psychological type and archetypes.

This partnership with CAPT would not have occurred without the vision of Katharine Myers, who brought us together. I appreciate her commitment to the larger context of Jungian studies, as well as psychological type, and for her encouragement.

I also am greatly indebted to my collaboration with Margaret Mark in *The Hero and the Outlaw: Building Extraordinary Brands through the Power of Archetype*. Discussions with her helped me fine-tune the Awakening the Heroes Within twelve-archetype system so that it would work optimally in organizational applications. In addition, I appreciate publisher Bonnie Horrigan and the editorial team of *The Inner Edge: A Resource for Enlightened Business Practice*—Michael Toms, Dennis Jaffe, and Michelle Hopkins, as well as our contributors for enhancing my understanding of organizational dynamics. I appreciate, too, Type and Temperament publisher Bill Murray's early understanding of the importance of creating a system of archetypes, structured and clear enough to encourage its use in human, leadership, and organizational development. Special thanks also to my students in the Transformational Leadership Certificate Program at Georgetown University and at the Saybrook Graduate School and Research Center for continually stimulating my thought processes about leadership and organizational systems.

Most of all I want to thank John G. Corlett, who has been truly wonderful to work with on this project. I thoroughly enjoyed the collaboration and have great respect for his thorough understanding of organizational dynamics. I know the resulting book is richer than either of us could have created without the other.

— CAROL S. PEARSON

INTRO | DUCTION

During the past twenty-five years, the ideas of Swiss psychologist C. G. Jung have profoundly affected the contemporary workplace. Jung's concept of psychological types, shaped and made widely available by the *Myers-Briggs Type Indicator*® instrument, has helped innumerable organization members in countless organizations understand themselves and their workmates better—and as a result become more productive and more creative. His theory of archetypes, built into the *Pearson-Marr Archetype Indicator*™ (*PMAI*™) and the *Organizational and Team Culture Indicator*™ (*OTCI*™), have given many organizations vital insights into the unconscious psychodynamics swirling beneath day-to-day workplace events. And many other Jungian ideas, including the shadow, the anima/animus, projection, *participation mystique,* and the transcendent function, have worked their way into the vocabulary and practice of a growing number of organizational consultants. Absent to date, however, has been a systematic guide to understanding and working with organizations from a Jungian standpoint.

This book steps into that gap, working on two levels. On one level, the book develops a theoretical framework for analyzing the psychodynamic underpinnings of organizational culture. The framework grows out of the ideas of Jung and his principal followers; we call it *Jungian Organization Theory*. At the heart of this framework is the concept of the organizational psyche, which encompasses all of an organization's psychological processes, conscious and unconscious. We believe our model is firmly grounded in Jung's analytical psychology, even though—proceeding in the spirit of exploration—we may push beyond what Jung himself theorized.

On a second level, this book is about encountering and understanding the organizational soul. *Psyche* is a Greek word that means *mind*. But it also means *soul.* Jung deliberately chose this term for describing the totality of a person's psychological being to set his psychology apart from the approaches of those who strive to pursue psychology as a strictly rational undertaking. For Jung, questions of psychology were inextricably connected—in a totally nonsectarian way—to the most profound questions of humankind's spirituality. In our associations, together and separately, with the many organizations referred to in the following pages,

C. G. Jung's Analytical Psychology

Analytical—or Jungian— psychology departs from other psychologies with roots in the late nineteenth century on two important grounds. First, is its assertion that the *psych* in psychology refers not just to the mind—as Freud would have had it—but to a union of mind and soul that the Greeks called *psyche.* According to Jung, the psyche is the totality of all psychic functioning, conscious as well as unconscious. It includes both structures (the ego, including psychological type; the persona; the archetypal Self; the shadow; and the *anima/ animus*) and processes (the complexes, repression and denial, projection, and the possibility of life-long development toward psychological wholeness).

▸ ▸ ▸

In Jung's view, the archetypal Self is a full partner in the psyche, if not the senior partner.

Jung's second major departure from the generally accepted views of his time is his assertion that there is an unconscious realm of reality that all humans share. He calls it the *collective, or objective, unconscious* and views it as part of the inherited structure of the human brain. Jung posits that the collective unconscious contains universally recognized patterns of meaning—motifs and images that can spring up anew anytime, anywhere, independently of historical tradition or migration. He labels these patterns archetypes and suggests that there are as many archetypes as there are typical situations in life. They are engraved into our psychic constitutions as forms without content, serving humanity as a kind of psychological DNA.

we have come to sense that these same questions of spirituality and ultimate meaning play out at the organizational level.

Psyche means *butterfly,* as well. There is a translucent, gossamer, here-again-gone-again quality to the psyche which makes it hard to put under a microscope and that gives our knowledge about it a slippery quality. The terms and structures we lay out in this book are rooted in metaphor as well as in analogy. They are at best symbolic or emblematic of organizational reality. No one can ever hope to catch more than occasional glimpses of the organizational psyche. But in the pages that follow, we have constructed a framework for labeling and tracking these glimpses, so that we can connect the dots and begin to see the outlines of the larger picture.

A DIFFICULT STARTING POINT

Jung did not make it easy to undertake the creation of a Jungian Organization Theory. He had fundamental concerns about the impact of groups and organizations on the psychological health of individuals. Among several statements that point to his misgivings are the following:

> *"Resistance to the organized mass can be [effected] only by the man who is as well organized in his individuality as the mass itself."* [1]

> *"When a hundred clever heads join in a group, one big nincompoop is the result, because every individual is trammeled by the otherness of the others."* [2]

> *"Large political and social organizations must not be ends in themselves, but merely temporary expedients . . . like cancerous growth, they eat away man's nature as soon as they become ends in themselves and attain autonomy. From that moment they grow beyond man and escape his control; he becomes their victim and is sacrificed to the madness of an idea that knows no master . . ."* [3]

Until very recently Jung's concerns seem to have discouraged efforts to use his ideas to analyze and help organizations. Theoretical work in the Jungian (analytical psychology) tradition on the organization-as-a-whole level has lagged behind work on organizational psychodynamics done from other points of view—notably the Freudian.

So, why do we persist in the face of Jung's apparent bias? First, we now live in what political theorist Robert Presthus calls an "organizational society."[4] Large organizations are likely to influence most of our waking hours. Jung died before this phenomenon came to dominate Western societies. In a sense, he had the luxury of holding organizations at arm's length as he defended the needs of individuals. We no longer have that luxury. Many an organization member, personally on the road to individuation, has found his or her organization unsupportive of—even hostile to—personal development and unable or unwilling to collaborate with employees in creating new organizational models built on a partnership between organizations and their members. We believe this negative dynamic has taken a heavy toll in terms of organizational productivity and employee well-being.

Second, there are voices within the Jungian community calling for translating Jung's ideas from the arena of the individual to the arena of systems and societies. Chief among them is archetypal psychologist James Hillman, who asserts that "we continue to locate all symptoms universally within the patient rather than also in the soul of the world." He argues that "maybe the system has to be brought into line with the symptoms so that the system no longer functions as a repression of soul, forcing the soul to rebel in order to be noticed."[5] Seconding Hillman's challenge are a handful of Jungians who have come to believe, as we do, that organizations can actually become places that foster individuation.[6]

Third, although Jung showed little interest in groups and organizations, he did not close the door completely on exploring them within the framework of analytical psychology. Jung believed that the psyche stretched as far outward as it did inward. And he was particularly interested in understanding its relation to its environment.[7] This book aims to help its readers better understand the psyche in its broadest context—starting with the organization.

Fourth, Myers-Briggs type theory, which is based on Jung's work on psychological types, is already widely used within organizations, although often without being placed in the context of Jung's broader work. In order for practitioners to use the Myers-Briggs construct competently, ethically, and to best effect, we believe they need to understand where type fits into the broad sweep of Jung's ideas and where it fits into the larger dynamics of an organization's psyche.

Finally, we believe there is a hunger in organizations for ideas about creating more effective workplaces, ideas that go deeper than the usual bromides and flavor-of-the-month prescriptions. Simply put, we think there is much in Jung's thinking that can fundamentally change organizations for the better.

JUNGIAN ORGANIZATION THEORY IN CONTEXT

The Jungian Organization Theory laid out in this book draws from several fields of study. It builds directly, of course, on the work of a handful of scholars who previously have addressed discrete elements of the organizational psyche from a Jungian point of view.[8] And it obviously draws heavily on analytical psychology itself, as well as on the closely related field of archetypal psychology. The development of our concepts has also been influenced by six other fields of thinking and research, with which our ideas share some key assumptions. Five are in the arena of organizational science: organization development;[9] Sociodynamic Culture Theory;[10] Psychoanalytic Organization Theory;[11] Eclectic Psychodynamic Organization Theory;[12] and organizational transformation.[13] The sixth is transpersonal psychology.[14]

With Sociodynamic Culture Theory, organization development, and organizational transformation, Jungian Organization Theory shares the belief that the question of meaning—why organization members are willing to invest so much of their creativity and agency in organizations—is bound up in the collectively held values at the heart of an organization's culture. With Psychoanalytic Organization Theory and Eclectic Psychodynamic Organization Theory, Jungian Organization Theory shares the belief that meaning is deeply connected to unconscious dynamics in organizations—the unknown and unseen psychic forces that bind people to each other and to their work. With transpersonal psychology, Jungian Organization Theory shares the belief that these unconscious dynamics are animated and ennobled by the soul energy embodied in the archetypes and the collective unconscious.

Jungian Organization Theory takes a clear position on the long-standing debate about reification: whether an organization can be considered to have qualities belonging to the whole. Simply put, our organizational psyche model views the organization as an autonomous whole, with an existence, goals, and interests independent of its members. We take this stand for two reasons. First, our own experience in and of groups and organizations convinces us that there are phenomena that we simply cannot explain in any other way—e.g., the *as if* behavior of groups and the unconscious and unspoken norms that nonetheless get precisely transmitted to an organizational newcomer. Second, we believe that the hypothesis of the collective unconscious implies collective dynamics that can have group or organizational boundaries, as well as individual, societal, and cultural ones.[15]

WHO THIS BOOK IS FOR

It is our hope that this book will speak to several kinds of people:

Enquiring minds that find that traditional, rational models of organization leave too many questions about organizational life unanswered—questions about meaning, adaptiveness, integrity, and community. It is also for people who have come to suspect that the answers to these questions may lie in the irrational side of organizational life.

Organization development and human resource practitioners, whom we envision using this work as a primer on Jungian concepts and as a guide to diagnosing and intervening in organizations from a Jungian standpoint to help those organizations become more productive and creative. Many of these professionals have been applying bits and pieces of Jung's thinking to their work for some years, particularly psychological type, and many may also be familiar with Carol Pearson's work on archetypes in workplaces.[16] These practitioners have not until now, however, had at their disposal a systematic application of Jung's ideas to the organization.

Jungian analysts whose thoughts are turning to an organizational practice. We hope they might be inspired by the book to use their considerable experience with individuals as a powerful analogy for working with organizations.

Academicians and students in the fields of organization development, human resource management/development, organizational behavior, and organization theory. We think they will find that this book adds some fresh insights to the literature on organizational culture theory from the psychodynamic point of view.

Entrepreneurs in the start-up phase of an organization's life, who want to insure organizational health and vitality from the beginning, and who recognize the incredible power and force of first causes in the long-term success of any endeavor.

Managerial leaders who are open to new ideas for improving the effectiveness of their organizations, democratizing the workplace, and re-energizing their work processes. Even if they know comparatively little about Jung and work in organizations where Jungian ideas are quite foreign, we believe they will find encouragement in the book to put more trust in the members of their organizations and to move from being guardians of the answers to being keepers of the questions.

Organization members—with some knowledge of typology and other Jungian ideas-who are looking for ideas to help them cope with the day-to-day frustrations of organizational life and ways to influence changes that can make their workplaces saner and more fulfilling places in which to spend time.

All persons who are striving to re-member the fragmented psyches of the organizations in which they work, to create soul-full workplaces that can welcome as partners the individuating people who populate them.

HOW TO USE THIS BOOK:
MAPPING *YOUR* ORGANIZATION'S PSYCHE

We think that the way to get the most out of this book is to apply it as you go. We invite you now to identify an organization you know well and one whose well-being matters to you. Your relationship to this organization could be empowered member, managerial leader, or consultant. The relationship may be current or past.

With your chosen organization in mind, we suggest that you map its psyche by working through the questions and tasks in part two of the book. We will cue you from time to time as the book unfolds to stop and do some work. Taken together, these questions and the associated diagrams and worksheets will help you use Jungian Organization Theory to systematically assess the psychological state of the organization, to consider a range of interventions for making it a healthier place, and to help you reflect on the nature of your relationship with your organization. (The cases in chapter 6 show how we have used these same questions in our work with various organizations.) Bear in mind as you proceed that Jung-oriented organizational assessment is rational only up to a point. It embraces conventional approaches to diagnosis where they apply. But, grounded in the belief that unconscious processes are a central reality of organizational life and that they must be dealt with if change efforts are to have lasting effect, organizational assessment from a Jungian stance also seeks to understand the irrational side of organizational life.

You may need some ancillary tools to do this work. Three of these—the *System Stewardship Survey*™, the *Archetypal Leadership Styles Survey*™, and the *Archetypes of Family Culture*™ chart—appear in the appendices. Three others—the *Myers-Briggs Type Indicator*®, the *Pearson-Marr Archetype Indicator*™, and the *Organizational Team Culture Indicator*™ instruments—are available through the Center for Applications of Psychological Type (see resources).

Notes

1. Jung (1957, p. 72).

2. Illing (1957, pp. 78-83) quotes personal correspondence with Jung.

3. Jung (C.W. 10, para. 719).

4. Presthus (1978; cited by Morgan, 1986, p. 112).

5. Hillman and Ventura (1992, p. 154).

6. See, for example, Stein and Hollwitz (1992, p. viii).

7. Capra (1982, p. 360).

8. See, for example, Stein and Hollwitz (1992); Bridges (1992).

9. See, for example, Weisbord (1987).

10. See, for example, Schein (1985); Alevesson (1990); Allen et al. (1987).

11. See, for example, De Board (1978); Diamond (1993).

12. See, for example, Marshak and Katz (1994); Morgan (1986); Krefting and Frost (1985).

13. See, for example, Levy and Merry (1986); Quinn and Cameron (1988).

14. See, for example, Grof (1988); Assagioli (1965).

15. The debate about reification is an old one in organization theory circles. For views that tend to support our own, see, for example, Argyris (1964); Schein (1985); Sinclair (1993, pp. 63, 70); Grof (1985, p. 127 and 1988, pp. 45–73); Stein and Hollwitz (1992); Morgan (1986, p. 224); Marshak and Katz (1990, pp. 58–59); and Krefting and Frost (1985, p. 161). For the antireification position, see, among others, Weber (cited by Silverman, 1971, pp. 140–1); Allport (1933, p. 234); and Silverman (1971, p. 9).

16. See various works by Pearson and Mark and Pearson.

THE Bat, the Bramblebush and the Gull:
A Fable by Aesop

The story that follows speaks to us from the sixth century, BCE. As you read it, listen for the surprisingly modern notes it sounds about contemporary organizational life.

> A Bat, a Bramblebush, and a Gull agreed to form a business partnership. The Bat borrowed money to provide capital, the Bramblebush acquired cloth, and the Gull supplied a lot of copper ingots. They hired a ship and departed home to peddle their goods overseas. After some days at sea, the ship encountered a sudden squall, capsized, and sank. The three partners escaped unharmed, but all their merchandise went down. For years after the disaster, the Gull haunted the shoreline, hoping that some of his copper might wash up on the beach; the Bat, terrified that the man who held his note might find him, remained out of sight during the day, coming out of his cave only at sundown; and the Bramblebush stood in lonely vigil along a path, snagging the garments of passing travelers to find out if any of the cloth in their garments might once have been his.[1]

1

Aesop seems *not* to have offered a moral for this fable. Here's our idea of a possible moral: if the answer lies *in here,* you won't find it by looking *out there.*

The story is rich in metaphors and symbols that point to a depth psychology interpretation. The ship, a symbol for the enterprise, sets out on its business. It encounters adversity in the form of the storm (sounds like white water). It capsizes and dumps the partners and their goods, symbolic of their wholeness, into the water, symbolic of the unconscious. The partners escape with their lives but lose their goods. They are alive but not whole, unaware of what has been plunged into the unconscious. The Bat, the Bramblebush, and the Gull spend the rest of their lives—and by extrapolation the life of the partnership—searching for their goods (wholeness) *out there* (on the periphery, in the shadow, in isolating denial) rather than *in here* (in the unconscious). All three are in a kind of trancelike state that produces a great deal of *as if* activity, i.e., actions based on the assumption that something is true that is not. In order to return themselves and their organization to a healthy place, they need instead to be looking for their goods in the sea (unconscious) and striving to reconnect their lives with their goods.

Suffice it to say, the fable paints an all-too-common picture, that of an organization in the grips of its unconscious stuff rather than living in partnership with it. Most of us have lived through some version of this tale. We engage in planning, clarify our collective vision, values, and mission, and set goals. We then metaphorically set out to sea. Next, all hell breaks loose. Of course, something happens that was not in the plan. Living as we do in permanent white water, something unexpected *always* happens. But then something *else* occurs, which is what makes this turbulence fatal. Everyone starts acting out, individually and collectively. They fight, or project on others, or go into denial, or engage in any number of neurotic behaviors that undermine the success of the voyage. The organization may technically stay afloat, but its members feel lost, at sea, as if they have been shipwrecked. What do they do? They go to the *periphery* and look for answers outside the organization. They pick at each other or their leadership. Or they retreat and become territorial and reclusive.

What we have come to see is that anytime the conscious mind commits to a grand adventure, the unconscious shows us what needs to be healed in order for that journey to be successful. However, if we do not understand this, the unconscious, irrational nature of the inevitable display derails the enterprise. As a result the organization loses touch with its unconscious parts. Huge quantities of human energy (libido) are lost, hidden, blocked, or ignored in organizations such as the fabled one—

energy that is not then available for creative and generative activities.

This book is written to help you chart your organization's course in a way that acknowledges the unconscious as well as the conscious aspects of the organization and its journey. Following this course, we believe, can help organizations avoid the many forms that the "shipwreck" takes in the contemporary world of organization: from chronic financial weakness to low morale; from unethical behavior to illegal practices.

Notes

1. Adapted from Levine's translation (1975, p. 10).

PART | ONE

Surveying
THE Organizational
Psyche

CHAPTER ONE

THE Organizational Psyche: An Overview

The concept of the organizational psyche that we explore in this book grows out of an analogy: the psyche of a human organization is like the psyche of a human individual. We develop the analogy based on our own experience with organizations and with the help of C. G. Jung and numerous thinkers and writers who have followed in his footsteps.

Jung was an early and prominent system thinker.[1] His insights into human systems at the individual level, particularly the idea that the collective unconscious provides a basic link between the individual and humanity as a whole, led us to envision the organizational psyche as a relatively open system, having these elements:

- an environment (including the collective unconscious);
- a semi-permeable boundary encompassing the whole;
- an interactive relationship between the organizational psyche and its environment; semi-autonomous subparts (conscious and unconscious dimensions, each with multiple elements);
- dynamic relationships among the subparts (the natural interplay of conscious and unconscious elements and forces);
- and the capacity for self-creation, self-regulation, and self-renewal (embedded in the organization's soul).

FIGURE 1 *The Individual Psyche*

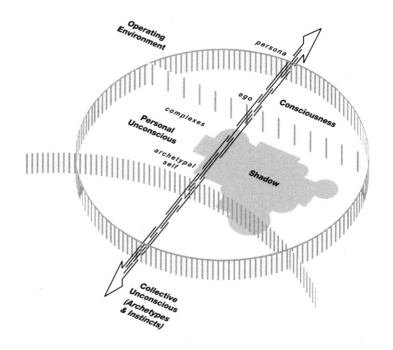

The parts of our model of the organizational psyche are analogous to the structures and elements Jung envisioned as aspects of the individual human psyche (see figure 1): consciousness and the unconscious, archetypal self, ego, persona, and the shadow. (See glossary.) The dynamics of our organizational model mirror those Jung saw in the inner lives of the individuals who were his clients: repression and denial, projection, complexes, dreams and other archetypal stirrings, the reciprocal balancing and rebalancing of conscious and unconscious energy (represented in figure 1 by the two-head arrow), synchronicities, and the movement over the life span toward psychological wholeness.[2]

BALANCE IN MOTION

Above all, our concept of the organizational psyche is influenced by Jung's thinking about psychic energy. Reduced to its simplest terms, the organizational psyche is an energy system powered by the libido—the same libido, or psychic energy, that Jung saw as an expression of the basic dynamics of life in individuals. As in the arena of physical energy, bipolarity is central to the concept of psychological energy. The tension of the opposites creates, distributes, and redistributes the psychic energy. Jung saw this dynamic as analogous to the process of physiological equilibrium, noting "if a given quantity of psychic energy is expended or consumed in bringing out a certain condition, an equal quantity of the same or another form of energy will appear elsewhere."[3]

For example, the polar opposite of the energy of creation is that of destruction. If these are in balance in the psyche of an organization, the organization's productive processes will be constantly reinvigorated as change (the new replacing the old) takes place. However, if the decision makers in the organization believe in creation, but not destruction, the latter will take up residence in the organization unconscious, where it is likely to fuel self-destructive behaviors. The organization will continually shoot itself in the foot. Or, as explained in Jung's notion of synchronicity (or meaningful coincidence), the organization will find itself drawn into situations where a serious threat comes from without. Such events may include shifts in economic or market realities that threaten the organization's sustainability, technological breakthroughs that make its major products or services obsolete, or costly legal entanglements (such as an antitrust suit or being called up for violations of equal opportunity or safety regulations) which distract from the work at hand and undermine the esteem in which the organization is held, within and without.

This dialectical relationship of conscious and unconscious organizational energies is crucial to a Jungian understanding of organizational dynamics. The conscious part of organizational life focuses on the "what" of business, downplaying the "why" or answering the "why" in superficial ways (to make our goals, to satisfy our benefactors, to make a profit). The unconscious aspect of organizational life provides real juice to fuel the organization, energy that comes from peoples' deeper motivations, which range from rather primal urges (like revenge) to rather sublime ones (like benefiting the planet). In between are desires to make one's parents proud, to outperform a sibling, to seem powerful and attractive to a lover, or to demonstrate mastery in tangible ways that result in self-esteem.

If the *unconscious* urges are not engaged, the organization will ignite no fire in the bellies of its members. Yet, if those urges are not then channeled by the conscious mind into productive activity, they can work at odds with the stated goals of the organization. This is apparent, for example, when peoples' aggressive instincts are siphoned off into office turf battles, inappropriate office affairs, or other soap opera dramas, instead of helping energize the fulfillment of the organization's goals.

In the organizational psyche (see figure 2), the system of energy is fed by the fundamental human will—which has both conscious and unconscious dimensions—to achieve, relate, meet basic needs, and learn. Organizational processes gather, shape, and direct this energy for the organization's purposes. When the system is in tune with itself, there is a continual ebbing and flowing of energy between conscious organizational life and the organization unconscious. This self-regulating, back-and-forth flow of energy produces a kind of dynamic homeostasis.

FIGURE 2 *The Organizational Psyche*

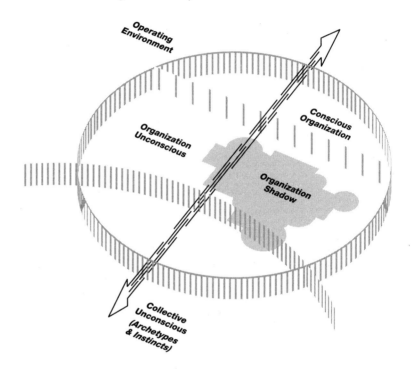

Conscious intent (one might think of this as free will) has a role in programming the unconscious and asking for its help. However, so does griping in the halls, which reinforces peoples' fascination with drama ("psyche, give me more intrigue"), not to mention leftover injunctions from parents (working hard makes you a good child). The unconscious helps consciousness get what it wants by establishing the polarities; expressing them in dreams, symptoms, and intuitive hunches; and giving hints to consciousness about ways it might expand or deepen its conscious desires—especially if its goals are out of line with its fundamental nature, capabilities, or circumstances.

When the self-regulating processes in the organizational psyche go awry, the resulting polarization can essentially cut off the organization from itself, its head from its body, consciousness from the unconscious. In these circumstances the organization unconscious can engender organizational errors, poor morale, low productivity, stunted creativity, and the profound disaffection of organization members. As in the fable, it can also cut the organization off from reality, causing it to live as *if* its projections about itself and the world were true. Or, both consciousness and the unconscious can engender action, but in separate, uncoordinated ways that result in situations analogous to Marx Brothers routines. People expend a good bit of energy running this way and that, but the outcome is that they just keep bumping into each other and never really get anywhere.

This book assumes—as does the process of Jungian analysis for individuals—that a kind of alchemy results when the conscious mind of an organization becomes aware of the organization's unconscious contents and is able to partner with the power found there. When this happens, the conscious organizational mind also has a regulating function, learning from unconscious energies and then aligning them to help achieve outcomes that are responsible and profitable (in for-profit organizations) or sustainable (in not-for-profits).

In a healthy organization, one where the members recognize the reality of both the conscious and unconscious parts of the organizational psyche, energy moves freely along the axis, or two-ended arrow, we have drawn in figure 2. Signs of this free movement of energy include the ability of organizational leaders to track reality accurately enough for business success, communication and morale that are at least adequate to support high productivity, and a general sense among organizational members of engagement with their work. This vibrancy grows out of the interplay between an organization unconscious that—when allowed to do its work—can readily provide the necessary counterbalance to conscious organizational processes and conscious processes that—cognizant of the potential contribution of the unconscious—can easily provide the necessary outlet for unconscious energies.[4] Neither of the two parts, in short, can achieve full expression without the participation of the other. If consciousness is the flower, then the unconscious is the root. It may, in fact be more useful to think of consciousness and the unconscious as ends of a continuum. Always bearing in mind the essential interpenetration of these two realities, we will undertake detailed explorations of the two poles in separate chapters. In chapter 2, we will examine the unconscious pole of this organizational energy system. In chapter 3, we will consider the conscious pole.

Notes

1. Capra (1982, p. 359ff).

2. Corlett (1996).

3. Jung (C.W. 7, para.115 and 1965, p. 209); Mattoon (1981, pp. 105, 108, 111); and Jacobi (1965, pp. 13, 14, 53–54) view polarity as the basis of psychic energy. Energy

flows in the psyche by virtue of the difference in potentials between the ego and the self, consciousness and the unconscious.

4. Jacobi (1965, pp. 54–5, 91); Beebe (1992); and Stein (in Stein and Hollwitz, 1992) describe the "ego-self axis" as the primary mechanism by which the self-regulation of the individual psyche takes place. This set of ideas was useful in helping us conceptualize the energy axis between organizational consciousness and the organization unconscious as the psychological spine of organizational life.

CHAPTER TWO

THE Organizational Psyche: The Unconscious Realm

Before we move into the main topic of this chapter, a note of explanation is in order. We begin our exploration of the organizational psyche with its unconscious dimension out of our belief that the unconscious predates and precedes consciousness and remains the more powerful. Like individuals, organizations evolve psychologically out of the vast reservoir of inchoate humanness that is the collective unconscious. We see the organizational journey as moving from unconsciousness to consciousness, and, like a tugboat pushing an ocean liner, conscious organizational processes are always dwarfed by their unconscious counterparts.

The unconscious realm of the organizational psyche has three main aspects. One of them, the collective unconscious, is a concept that lies at the heart of analytical psychology. The other two, the organization unconscious and the Archetype of Organization, are extensions of C. G. Jung's theories, which we believe have utility in understanding organizational psychology. The organization unconscious parallels the personal unconscious in an individual and has analogous attributes. The Archetype of Organization parallels the archetypal Self in the individual.

THE COLLECTIVE UNCONSCIOUS

The collective unconscious undergirds the organizational psyche, just as it

FIGURE 3 *The Organizational Psyche*

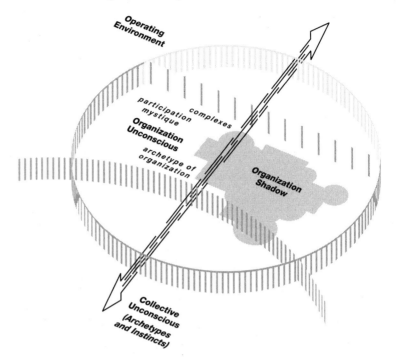

undergirds the individual psyche. It is a "psychic system of a universal and impersonal nature which is identical for all individuals, all groups, and all organizations. The collective unconscious does not develop individually, but originates in the inherited structure of the brain."[1] In a sense, the collective unconscious is the container of our most basic memories as a race and serves as the foundation of humankind's shared sense of what it means to be human.

Jung suggested that the collective unconscious has two kinds of contents: first, the instincts, which are "uniform and regularly recurring modes of action"; second, the archetypes, which are "uniform and regularly recurring modes of apprehension." The archetypes are "mythological associations, motifs and images, of which we can become conscious only indirectly. They can spring up anew anytime, anywhere, independently of historical tradition or migration."[2] There are probably as many archetypes as there are typical human experiences. Archetypes can be understood as patterns of psychic energy impressed onto the racial memory. Post-Jungians have described the archetypes variously as the "structural elements of the collective unconscious," the "pictorial forms of the instincts," "unconscious psychological entities comparable to the invisible presence of the crystal lattice in a saturated solution," and "the link between sense perception and ideas."[3]

14

We agree with organizational scientist Morley Segal's assertion that archetypes are "key contributors to organizational culture, many of them representing the forms or outlines of the basic responses to organizational life."[4] But we go a step further to suggest that the archetypes and the collective unconscious as a whole make up a psychological field that serves as the deep foundation of an organization's culture, supporting its dynamic and continually interactive motion like the giant rollers built into the deepest substructures of earthquake-resistant buildings.

THE ORGANIZATION UNCONSCIOUS

The organization unconscious is the analog in the organizational psyche for the personal or subjective unconscious.[5] It is the set of unconscious psychological energies, contents, and truths unique to a particular organization that operates beyond the conscious control and awareness of those who manage and lead the organization. It is the realm of unconscious psychic activity in an organization that lies between the conscious life of the organization and the collective unconscious. Jung did not posit the existence of the organization unconscious, but we believe he left the door open to the development of this idea by implying—in his work on family complexes—the existence of a "family unconscious" and in his assertion that the psyche has a collective aspect.[6] The organization unconscious—a complex web of usually unseen and unrecognized energy vectors—provides the psychological subflooring of organizational culture, at times supporting, at times frustrating organizational life.[7] In a sense, the organization unconscious provides a psychodynamic arena in which the conscious organization and the collective unconscious can meet.

We think the existence of the organization unconscious can be inferred from the irrationality of the social attachments that bind organizations together; from the inexplicable actions (e.g., the Challenger disaster) and inactions (e.g., the persistence of racism) that haunt the corridors of most, if not all, organizations; from the dark humor—prevalent in so many organizations—that wells up out of all that has been repressed; and from the little miracles and synchronicities that sometimes bless organizations when least expected, e.g., the sudden emergence, seemingly from nowhere, of a *third* way that ends a bitter dispute.

The organization unconscious has three primary elements or contents. First, the organization shadow, which comprises all the facets and dimensions of the organization collectively repressed because they do not fit the set of attitudes, preferences, and behaviors deemed appropriate by those who make the organization's rules and establish its procedures and values. One example of shadow contents is the organization where the conscious processes are dominated by masculine forms and mores, and the feminine principle is repressed into the organization shadow. This may be the case at General Electric, where for years the company has struggled with a poor reputation when it comes to hiring and promoting women[8]; and where, of the thirty-one top executives in late 2000, only one was a women.[9] Another content of the organizational shadow is often the psychological type functions—thinking, feeling, intuition, or sensation—not preferred by the organization. The organization shadow—a kind of organizational alter ego—is largely out of the awareness of those who run an organization; but it can be quite obvious to outsiders and oftentimes to members of the organization who embody one or more of the values and qualities that have been repressed. In a sense, the organization shadow is the organization's dark/unrevealed/un-integrated side. It is important to remember that the organization shadow contains positive as well as negative potentials. (For more on the formation of the organization shadow, see the discussion of the organizational ego—we call it the center of consciousness—in chapter 3.)

The second component of the organization unconscious is the aggregate or nexus of projections made by the organization onto its members and by the members onto the organization. Each organization member has an unconscious connection to the organization that Jung called the *participation mystique*.[10] This dynamic meets the organization's unconscious need to attract individuals who can fill certain archetypal roles, while meeting the unconscious needs of its members to enact these roles. The archetypal structure of an organization will attract similarly minded people like a magnet attracting iron filings. The Hero archetype (also known as the Warrior), for example, is a dominant motif in the psyches of armies, and individuals in whom the same archetype is active will find themselves at home in military organizations, often without knowing why they feel so comfortable. The fit is good because the individuals and the organization are living the same archetypal story.[11]

The mutual, unconscious attraction of a man and a woman that underlies marriage may be an apt analogy for *participation mystique*. It is not uncommon, however, for a marriage to founder on the unconscious expectations the partners have of each other. So, too, an organization and its members may suffer if there is no awareness and acknowledgment of this unconscious dynamic. The organization may be limited in its ability to tap the creativity of its members, while the members may feel abused by reason of being pigeonholed. A woman might be drawn unconsciously to a job where her inclination to *be in charge* can have scope, but she may at some point become exhausted, burned out and—because of this—

resentful over the organization's casual assumption that she can *always* be depended upon to *make things happen.*

The third component of the organization unconscious is the arena in which the day-to-day activities of an organization engage the energy of the archetypes and create *organizational complexes.* Organizational complexes are part of the normal psychic landscape of the organization unconscious. They *just are.* Moreover, they are a principal means by which the everyday patterns of organizational life—the organization's *doing* energy—are energized by the archetypal *being* energy of the collective unconscious.[12]

All organizations have complexes, as do some organizational sub-elements that have strong, independent identities. Normal complexes contribute to an organization's uniqueness. They are key building blocks of an organization's culture, often influencing the archetypal *story* that an organization lives out. A university department, for example, has a healthy Sage complex that has helped the department remain a place of high quality teaching, even as a decline in funding has increased class size and put additional bureaucratic burdens on faculty members. Without normal organizational complexes, i.e., complexes that do not distract the organization from its productive business, an organization would be significantly limited in its ability to tap into the archetypal energies flowing in the collective unconscious.

Organizational complexes come into being through a process not unlike that by which complexes become a part of the individual psyche: the organization has a collective emotional experience that resonates with a particular archetype, activating—or constellating—the archetype in the psyche of the organization. Over time, memories, thoughts, and feelings about the experience continue to well up in the organization, surrounding the constellated archetype with a web of psychic energy. A complex is born. Example: an organization establishes good employee benefits and policies that guarantee lifelong employment. Employees feel grateful and secure. These events constellate in the organization unconscious the energy of the Caregiver or nurturing mother. Over time, stories and myths accumulate in the organization about employees *being taken care of* and about the organization *being there* when employees are in need. The organization has developed a Caregiver complex. Before globalization forced widespread downsizing and streamlining in the 1980s and 1990s, many a company had a version of this complex, as well as the culture of entitlement that often accompanied it.

Organization members clearly are aware of the stories and myths that fuel the development of a complex. They are typically unaware, however, of the psychological dynamic that welds these stories into an energy dynamo whirring away in the organization unconscious. This process goes on endlessly in the life of all organizations.[13] The tip-off to the existence of an organizational complex is the existence of an unusually high level of shared emotion among organization members about a particular issue or set of issues.

THE ARCHETYPE OF ORGANIZATION DEFINED

We have come to believe that there is an underlying purposefulness in organizational psychodynamics. We share with several other scholars the view that the human inclination to create organizations is the expression of an archetype.[14] The existence of this archetype means that all organizations share a deep meaning and intentionality that lie beyond the sway of the egos of individual organizational members. This organizational archetype lives at the psychological heart of all organizations, making each organization broadly the same as all the others. At the same time, the specific complexes, culture, processes, structure, goals, and environment of any particular organization combine to make it unique. Organizations are nothing if not paradoxes!

We call this underlying archetype the *Archetype of Organization*. We see this archetype as a very rough organizational analogy for Jung's concept of the archetypal Self in the psyche of the individual. He viewed the arche-

FIGURE 4 *The Archetype of Organization*

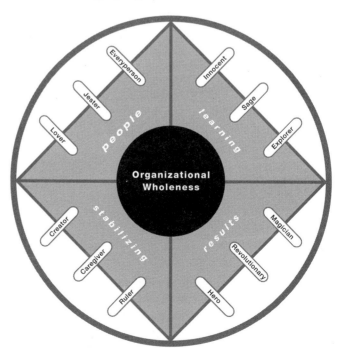

typal Self as the "archetype of orientation and meaning,"[15] "both the center and periphery of the individual psyche."[16] In much the same way, the Archetype of Organization serves as a significant source of and as the channel of organizational energy. It embodies much of an organization's innate capacity for wholeness.

In the paradoxical Jungian worldview, the Archetype of Organization is a part of the organization's psychic system; but it also stands for the psychic system as a whole. As the psychological core of the organization, the Archetype of Organization is the template of organizations, in general, of the human desire to band together in a purposeful way. It is the primary vehicle through which the collective unconscious speaks to an organization, urging it to develop toward completeness. It lies at the heart of an organization's sense of itself. The Archetype of Organization points the organization toward what it can become, providing a blueprint for wholeness. As the psychological boundary of an organization, the Archetype of Organization is the full and unique expression of a particular organization in dialogue with its environment. It serves as a container for the organization's learning and development.[17]

The Archetype of Organization becomes constellated in an organization at the moment the partners shake hands on the deal—as did the Bat, the Bramblebush, and the Gull, or at the moment the articles of incorporation are signed. From that time on, the members of an organization collectively and unconsciously carry the Archetype of Organization into the psychodynamic life of an organization, and it becomes imperfectly manifest through them and their actions—both individual and collective, both conscious and unconscious.

We suggest that the Archetype of Organization has a mandala-like structure. At its core, four great life forces come together in two sets of polar opposites.[18] The first pair of archetypal life forces consists of the tendency to nurture and develop *People*, in tension with the tendency to achieve *Results*. The second pair consists of the tendency toward *Learning*, innovating and transforming, in tension with the tendency toward *Stabilizing* processes and maintaining tradition.[19]

Each of the four life forces has three human faces or forms by which we typically recognize them and through which we most often encounter these archetypal energies as they flow through organizational life. *People* energy is carried and channeled by the archetypal images of the Everyperson, the Lover, and the Jester; *Results* energy by the Hero, the Revolutionary, and the Magician; *Learning* energy by the Innocent, the Explorer, and the Sage; and *Stabilizing* energy by the Caregiver, the Creator and the Ruler. Each of the twelve faces has the potential for both a feminine and a masculine style of expression. And each has a dark or demonic side.

▶ ▶ ▶

THE TWELVE HUMAN FACES
OF THE ARCHETYPE OF ORGANIZATION

The PEOPLE *Faces: Three Styles of Relating and Belonging*

Everyperson demonstrates the virtues of simply being an ordinary person, just like everybody else. It links us to the Everyperson figure in the medieval morality plays, the ideas of the common person in political theory, and the emotional impact of the Tomb of the Unknowns. The dark side of the Everyperson includes scapegoating, going along to get along, and vulnerability to faddishness. Everyperson organizations tend to treat everyone the same but no one very well and dress is often blue-collar in style. Generally, these organizations share a strong belief in the importance of each individual and are disinclined to engage in heroine or hero worship to single out anyone as particularly special or worthy.

The Lover helps us connect, form relationships, and be intimate with others. It helps us let go of narrow self-interest and to act in concert to be more than we could be alone. The dark side of the Lover includes emotional drama, over-emphasis on consensus, and cliquishness. Lover organizations are likely to operate in a democratic, consensual manner and to like cooperative and worker-owned structures. Feelings, emotional honesty, beauty, and closeness with co-workers and customers are valued.

The Jester knows how to foster a spirit of lightness and play. If others are combative, the Jester can play at war. If people are being hurt, the Jester moves on to something more enjoyable. The Jester lightens people up so they can have a good time. The dark side of the Jester includes black humor, con artistry, and disregard for norms and mores. Jester organizations value spontaneity, newness, fun, and innovation. They have little tolerance for forms, policies, formal structure, or bureaucratic procedures.

The RESULTS *Faces: Three Paradigms for Maximizing Results*

The Hero wants to make the world a better place. The Hero's underlying fear is failing to have what it takes to persevere and prevail. This energy helps develop vitality, discipline, focus, and determination. The dark side of the Hero includes arrogance, the need for an enemy, ruthlessness, and obsessive need to win. Hero organizations often are either committed to a worthwhile cause or devoted to helping their customers and employees to be all that they can be. Standards are high, and employees are expected to do whatever it takes to succeed.

The Revolutionary holds the values of the counterculture—past, present, or future. The goal of the Revolutionary is to foment change, to destroy what is not working, or to even the playing field by radically changing or breaking the rules. The dark side of the Revolutionary includes criminal or evil behavior. In Revolutionary organizations everything is up for grabs. Nothing and no one has privilege based on position or on the past.

The Magician channels inspiration and intuition into concrete reality. The Magician strives to transform lesser realities into better realities, often by introducing a third element into a situation, thus moving beyond dualistic thinking. The dark side of the Magician includes manipulative behavior, lack of continuity, and being too far ahead of one's time. Magician organizations are highly energized, focused, flexible, innovative, and quick to respond to change. They are extraordinarily adaptive in the face of changing circumstances.

The LEARNING *Faces: Three Approaches to Change and Growth*

The Innocent is simple, trusting, and good—often seeking guidance and insight from others or expecting an authority figure to be the teacher. The Innocent expresses itself in an optimism that transcends the apparent facts of the situation and manifests itself in activities related to reinvention, reframing, and renewal. The dark side of the Innocent includes the potential for victimization, masochistic behavior, and denial. Innocent organizations are benevolent, highly hierarchical, and centralized. Managers function like caring parents, and employees deport themselves like well-behaved children.

The Explorer goes out seeking a better world. The Explorer pursues new experiences and things as a means of determining self-identity in the context of new possibilities and options. The Explorer may also be known as the seeker, iconoclast, wanderer, or individualist. The dark side of the Explorer includes aimless wandering, or becoming a misfit. Explorer organizations value individuality, de-emphasize rules and hierarchical decision making, and tend to allow employees to control their time and workload. They tend to be flat and democratic, rewarding the achievement of goals however flexibly achieved.

The Sage seeks wisdom, striving to identify universal truths and to live in keeping with their mandates. The Sage creates clarity from chaos and claims some degree of mastery of the learning process. The dark side of the Sage includes pedantry, dogmatism, censoriousness, ivory tower syndrome, and lack of feeling for people. Sage organizations personify the concept of the learning organizations, continually seeking feedback from all sources and using it for greater internal integration and greater external adaptation. They value excellence, competence, planning, analysis, and clear logical thinking.

The STABILIZING *Faces: Three Stances on Structure*

The Caregiver nurtures others, tends the home fires, cares for the natural world, and focuses on structure in order to keep people safe. The Caregiver may be expressed in the pursuit of a healing profession, in the joy of developing a protégé, or in maintaining an orderly or attractive environment. The dark side of the Caregiver includes codependency, conflict avoidance, and martyrdom. Caregiver organizations are characterized by selflessness and service. Harmony, cooperation, and care are held to be basic institutional values.

The Creator converts imagination into creative application—art, inventions, developing innovative ideas or products. The Creator ennobles the human condition by contributing to the development of culture and focusing on structure to form new realities. The dark side of the Creator includes creativity without application, finding that nothing is good enough, and inattention to routine. Creator organizations provide members with great latitude to express their creativity. The value of the work takes precedence over the bottom line.

The Ruler governs the physical world, taking control of and responsibility for the creation of forms, systems, and policies in order to maintain a just, orderly, and prosperous world. The Ruler expresses itself through management and leadership, focusing on structure to exert power or control. The dark side of the Ruler includes oppressive behavior, sacrificing people for power, and cutting ethical corners. Ruler organizations are stable, productive, orderly, and quite bureaucratic. They function smoothly, with timely procedures and policies.[20]

▶ ▶ ▶

THE ARCHETYPE OF ORGANIZATION IN ACTION

Alone, none of the four life energies is sufficient for guiding and shaping an organization. Within the energy field of the Archetype of Organization, they exert a creative pull on each other, producing a rich alchemical soup that reins in each life energy from the excesses of its dark side and provides the necessary balance between masculine and feminine energies. Most organizations have an archetypal *story* in which one *face* (sometimes two faces) of the Archetype of Organization predominates, giving the organization a special character. But in psychologically healthy organizations at least one face of each of the four basic energies of the Archetype of Organization plays an important role in the psychodynamic life of the organization.

We see Southwest Airlines under CEO Herb Kelleher as a good example of how the Archetype of Organization informs an organization's culture. *People* energies in the form of the Lover highlight Southwest's archetypal story. Kelleher talks openly about love as his basic approach to leadership, and this ethic appears to run deep in the day-to-day flow of organizational life. Lover energy gives Southwest its defining brand identity. It provides, as does the primary archetypal face of every organization, the underlying sense of meaning to all stakeholders, that is, it explains *why* the organization does what it does. If company policies were to fly in the face of the organization's public statement of belief, both morale and credibility would suffer.

At Southwest, the archetypal story is also heavily influenced by a second face of the Archetype of Organization, the Jester. The appearance of a secondary face is not uncommon. When it shows forth, this auxiliary archetypal energy often defines an organization's ideal process, that is, *how* the organization likes to do its business. This is true at Southwest, where, having fun at work seems to rank close to the top of the list of corporate values.

The mandala structure of the Archetype of Organization allows these publicly claimed *People* faces to be complemented by generous measures of the other three life energies. *Results* energies are evident in the face of the Hero—Southwest had to claw its way into existence against the economic and legal opposition of established airlines and has remained strongly goal oriented. *Stabilizing* energies are evident in the face of the Ruler—Kelleher and his main lieutenant are forceful, take-charge leaders enforcing an underlying orderliness and attention to detail. *Learning* energies are evident in the face of the Explorer—Southwest has based its business model on pioneering a new concept, literally inventing the small-airport-to-small-airport business niche. At Southwest, as in most organizations, these balancing archetypes generally are less fully articulated, but they still play a powerful role in the culture of the organization. Indeed, they often define its unwritten rules. At Southwest, one of these unwritten rules appears to be *doing whatever it takes*, a value inspired by the Hero.

As just noted, these ancillary life energies form vital parts of the substructure of a culture characterized by genuine human warmth, hard-nosed business acumen, production process precision, and continuous change and adaptation.[21] Were the Archetype of Organization *not* at the center of Southwest's archetypal field channeling these secondary forces into a productive relationship with the dominant archetype motifs, the *Results, Stabilizing,* and *Learning* energies would tend to go underground, feeding a powerful and potentially destructive shadow.

In addition to the core archetype or archetypes, other archetypes related to an organization's stage of life (birth, growth, decline), to the exigencies of doing business, or to the personality of leaders will regularly become constellated in the lives of organizations; but in a healthy organization, the Archetype of Organization will serve as a kind of unconscious template, balancing energies and fostering wholeness. It keeps the organization from springing out of control by preventing any one archetype from having too much influence, channeling the energy of other archetypes into the psychic life of the organization, and shaping and moderating the archetypal field upon which the organization's culture rests.

Note, too, that various divisions and groups within an organization may differently stress the life energies of the Archetype of Organization or show a different human face than the organization as a whole. This is natural and healthy, as long as the difference is related to the appropriate function or mission of that particular group. During mergers and acquisitions, it can be useful to use the life energies of the Archetype of Organization as categories to help assess whether the organizational cultures of the merging organizations are compatible with one another.

ORGANIZATIONAL WHOLENESS

The paradoxical product of the tension between and among the four archetypal energies of the Archetype of Organization is what we call *organizational wholeness*. Roughly analogous to individuated wholeness for the individual psyche, *organizational wholeness*, or completeness, is the best an organization can hope to be—a way of being that is a full expression of the Archetype of Organization within a unique set of worldly realities. *Organizational wholeness* is the same for all organizations, inasmuch as it is always rooted in the four life forces. And it is different for each organization.

It is different by virtue of the fact that in each organization it is mediated by different faces of the Archetype of Organization. And it is different inasmuch as it is a function of an organization's values and preferred processes, of the psyches of an organization's founders and key stake-holders, and of the environment in which an organization is operating.

Authoritarian management can temporarily create a dangerously one-sided organization, thwarting the organization's movement toward *organizational wholeness*. Except in the most pathological situations, however, the Archetype of Organization will provide a corrective influence—like a magnet silently arranging metal filings into a balanced pattern. When people come together in organizations, they create a collective, inchoate potential for organizational completeness that needs only the slightest encouragement to take form. Whether their actions are conscious or unconscious, the people within a healthy organization will collectively and naturally tend to correct for imbalances, sometimes before they are noticeable.

MAPPING AN ORGANIZATION'S PSYCHE

We invite you now to begin using Jungian Organization Theory to map the psyche of an organization you know well and whose well-being matters to you. Turn to part two, answer the questions under task one/steps one and two, and record your answers on the accompanying worksheets.

Notes

1. Jung (*C.W. 6*, para. 842 and *C.W. 9, Part I*, paras. 88–90).

2. Jung (*C.W. 8*, para. 273; *C.W. 8*, para. 280; and *C.W. 6*, para. 842).

3. Neumann (1954, p. xv); Mitroff (1984, p. 84); and Stevens (1991, p. 74).

4. Segal (1997, p. 68).

5. Jung (*C.W. 6*, para. 842).

6. Kast (1992, p. 97); and Jung (*C.W. 7*, para. 235)

7. Jung (*C.W. 6*, para. 837); Singer (1972, p. 87); and Whitmont (1969, pp. 150, 163) provided insights into the nature of the subjective or personal unconscious that we found helpful in thinking about how to differentiate the contents of the organization unconscious.

Our conception of the organization unconscious embraces and ultimately moves beyond the thinking of Jung-oriented organization theorists who have gone before us. Stein (in Stein and Hollwitz, 1992, p. 5); Segal (1997, p. 61); Neumann (1954, pp. 421–423); and Auger and Arneberg (in Stein and Hollwitz, 1992, p. 46) each suggests the existence of something like an organization (or group) unconscious.

Our thinking about the organization unconscious was also shaped by the ideas of some non-Jungians. The statement by Allen et al. (1987, p. 4) that there is an "organizational unconscious" was a factor in pushing us to take the same stand against those who argue that there are only unconscious processes in organizations, not an organization unconscious per se. Marshak and Katz (1990, pp. 58–59); Krefting and Frost (1985,

p. 161); Morgan (1986, p. 224); and Denhardt (1981) all suggest that there is something approximating our notion of the organization unconscious.

Our definition of the organization unconscious—with its three aspects—stands in sharp contrast to the position held by Freudian organization theorists. Speaking for that school, Diamond (1993, p. 34) argues that, while there is unconscious life in organizations—the countless projections of the organization members onto each other, their leaders, and the external world, there is no organization unconscious per se. It is, of course, the concept of the collective unconscious that lay at the heart of the split between Freud and Jung. And it is the frame of reference provided by Jung's concept of the collective unconscious that supports our assertion that the organization unconscious is more than the sum of the unconscious energies of its individual members.

8. *Working Woman* (December 1992, pp. 58-61).

9. Walsh (2000).

10. Stein (in Stein and Hollwitz, 1992, p. 6); and Stein (1996a, pp. 67–72).

11. Stein (in Stein and Hollwitz, 1992, p. 10) suggests that *participation mystique* forms the psychological underpinnings for an organization's culture. We, however, see the entire organization unconscious, not just participation mystique, as the foundation of organizational culture.

12. Lepper (in Stein and Hollwitz, 1992, pp. 72–91) uses system theories to help explore how Jung's concept of the complex might throw light on the psychodynamics of the organization. She suggests that an organization and its members interpenetrate to create organizational complexes that are embedded in the organization's dynamic systems, both technical and human. Our concept of the organizational psyche—itself a system construct—builds on Lepper's ideas by positing the existence of subsystems in the organizational psyche, e.g., center of consciousness and Archetype of Organization, and anchoring the development of organizational complexes in their interaction.

13. Our thoughts about how organizational complexes might come into being were influenced by Whitmont (1969, pp. 57–72); Jacobi, 1959 (pp. x, 54–5); Singer (1972, pp. 37–8); and Mattoon (1981, pp. 116–7,127). They generally agree that the complex in the individual is a dynamic that links the personal unconscious and the collective unconscious; it is an unconscious locus of psychic energy consisting of the memory of an experience, an archetype evoked by that experience, and an accretion of feelings and memories bearing some relationship to the primary experience.

14. Pondy et al. (1983, pp. 27, 28).

15. Jung (1965, p. 199 and *C.W.* 6, paras.789, 790).

16. Jacobi (1965, p. 49).

17. The Archetype of Organization builds on the ideas about "organizational self" posited by Colman (in Stein and Hollwitz, 1992, p. 95). Colman describes the "organizational self" as the organization's deepest identity, what it seeks to become, the unfolding of its potential, its inexorable movement toward integration and wholeness.

Our thinking about the Archetype of Organization was also influenced by Wink (1986, pp. 4, 70, 71, 169). He comes at the issue of organizational meaning from the perspective of a biblical scholar trying to re-articulate the nonmaterialist cosmology of two thousand years ago. He posits the existence of "organizational angels" or spirits, which he sees as the determining forces of physical, psychic, and social existence. Angel is synonymous for the numinous interiority of created things. "What the ancients called the angel of a collective entity actually answers to an aspect of all corporate realities: they do have an inner spirit, though our culture has been trained to ignore it."

18. Support for our notion that the Archetype of Organization—as an analogy for the self—has a fourfold and mandala-like nature comes from Jung himself. Jung (*C.W.* 5, para. 550) suggested that the self has a four-fold nature and declared (*C.W. 9, Part I*, para. 715) that the "squaring of the circle could even be called an archetype of wholeness."

Elaborating on this point, Edinger (1972, pp. 4, 179, 211) suggests that the significance of the quaternity to Jung is basic to his whole theory of the psyche, both as regards its structure and its developmental goal.

As to our thoughts about the specific textures of the Archetype of Organization, we find connections between our ideas and those of several thinkers. Moore and Gillette (1993, pp. 231–241) assert that at the deepest level, world renewal and self-renewal have the same archetypal underpinnings, i.e., four kinds of libido or psychic energy: magician, warrior-amazon, lover, and king-queen. In their view, these are arranged in the archetypal self in two pairs of opposing tendencies: magician/king-queen and lover/warrior-amazon. In suggesting the existence of the Archetype of Organization, we are arguing that this same *four-channel* energy flows through organizations at the same time providing a more expansive definition of the archetypes involved. W. Thompson (1971, cited by Mitroff, 1989, p. 98) suggests that four archetypal characters can be construed as the basic building blocks of society and all institutions: hunter/warrior, shaman/medicine man, clown/fool, and chief, a formulation, that while useful, has a more masculine orientation than our system. Denison and Mishra (1995) see four traits as the primary variables of organizational culture: involvement, consistency, adaptability, and mission. As for Greek roots, our notion of four essential energies resonates in the four temperaments of Hippocrates: choleric, sanguine, phlegmatic, and melancholic.

19. Other writers have used different sets of words to describe these same four life forces. Pearson and Seivert (1995) use Water *(People)*, Fire *(Results)*, Earth *(Stabilizing)*, and Air *(Learning)*. Pearson (1999) uses People *(People)*, Results *(Results)*, Stability *(Stabilizing)*, and Expertise *(Learning)*. Mark and Pearson (2001) use Belonging and Enjoyment *(People)*, Risk and Mastery *(Results)*, Stability and Control *(Stabilizing)*, and Independence and Fulfillment *(Learning)*.

20. For more details on the twelve faces of the Archetype of Organization see Pearson (2002b) and Mark and Pearson (2001).

21. Tyler (1997).

CHAPTER | **THREE**

THE Organizational
Psyche:
The **Conscious**
Realm

The conscious realm of the organizational psyche is the arena where the ego-directed actions and behaviors of those who are in charge hold sway over productive activity and the shaping of the organization's culture. This is the zone of affairs dealt with exhaustively by conventional organization theory and management theory. There is, however, an aspect of this activity that cannot be seen through conventional lenses. An underlying texture, both collective and influenced by the unconscious, begins coming into focus when the observer adopts a Jungian perspective. This underlying texture has two principal *threads:* the center of consciousness and the organization's public face.

CENTER OF CONSCIOUSNESS

The conscious realm of the organizational psyche has a focal point, a web of ego-directed actions and ideas we call the center of consciousness. We see it as being loosely analogous to Jung's concept of the individual ego.[1] The center of consciousness is an organizational process, comprising the myriad conscious activities—reflecting, planning, controlling, coordinating, and implementing—necessary for managing the work of the organization. With its rational and logical orientation, the center of consciousness serves to channel the organization's psychic energy into productive action.[2]

FIGURE 5 *The Organizational Psyche: The Conscious Realm*

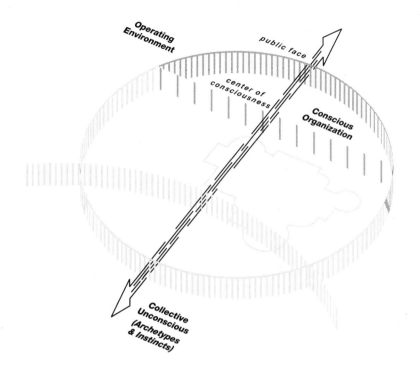

Embodied in people. The center of consciousness is embodied in the people and structures of the organization. In organizations where power and control are centralized, the center of consciousness may be essentially synonymous with a single person at the top. This was the case, for example, at Globe Metallurgical, Inc., when Arden C. Sims took over as chief executive officer in 1984. At that point, virtually every decision, whether engineering, metallurgical, or operational, funneled up to him.[3] In organizations where the CEO shares decision making with a top management group or team, that body will comprise the center of consciousness. In organizations moving toward more democratic ways of operating, the center of consciousness tends, however, to become embodied in a great many individuals and therefore more widely diffused throughout the organization.

Here are three examples of this diffusion:

- It began to happen at Ford Motor Company in the 1980s with the implementation of a widespread employee involvement/ participative management program.

- It took place at the Menninger clinic in the Midwest. During a period of several years, the clinic sent large numbers of its employees to Tavistock-style group relations conferences.

Reflecting on this later, the head of the clinic noted that this intervention had given his organization a kind of "observing ego," a new perspective and a new conceptual framework that had enabled the organization to grapple more effectively with the inevitable problems of organizational life.[4]

▸ It was the result at Whole Foods, Inc., where management created a team-based structure, opened up the books to the whole organization, and delegated decision making about the day-to-day operations to the teams.[5]

A quick and fairly reliable way to find out who constitutes the center of consciousness in any organization is to ask a member of the organization who *they* is.

In whatever way it is embodied, the center of consciousness has a clear sense of the work to be done and a set of beliefs about how the organization should operate in order to be productive and efficient. The center of consciousness becomes invested in vision and mission statements, statements of ethics, strategic plans, celebrations of organizational heroes, and declarations of values and creeds. The center of consciousness develops a coherent sense of itself and how to run the organization by choosing—more or less consciously—one set of values and approaches over another. The rejected values and approaches are thrust out of conscious consideration and become part of the organization shadow. The unconscious contents remain great potentials waiting to become important breakthroughs and great threats looking for ways to sabotage organizational life. (Refer back to the discussion of the organization shadow in chapter 2.)

Connection to the Archetype of Organization. The center of consciousness can potentially manifest—and in healthy organizations does manifest—all four dimensions of the energy that powers the Archetype of Organization (see chapter 2). But it is unlikely to do so as long as power is invested in only a few people who all look, think, and act much alike. An organization in which the center of consciousness becomes broadly invested in the organization's members is open to the energy field created by the interpenetration of all four of the energies of the Archetype of Organization: achieving *Results, Stabilizing* processes and systems, nurturing *People,* and *Learning* how to adapt and change. Such a center of consciousness tends to institutionalize curiosity, awareness, and the intentional seeking and using of feedback for continuous improvement. In a sense it becomes the much talked about *learning organization. Self-organization* is another contemporary management concept that can shed light on what an organization looks like when the center of consciousness includes a significant number of the organization's members. In an enterprise based on self-organization, executives, managers, and employees work together to develop a broad mission for the organization; and then all organization members—with the aid of streams of performance data—figure out how to get the job done.[6]

Masculine/feminine feel. The center of consciousness of an organization may have a predominantly masculine or feminine character. Jung used the terms masculine and feminine to describe archetypal principles, both of which reside in the psyches of both men and women. Masculine connotes power, meaning, structure, form, objectivity, product, and the abstract. Feminine connotes relatedness, conciliation, integration, subjectivity, service, and the concrete. Jung saw each principle as a necessary to complement the other, each as insufficient by itself.[7] We believe that these concepts can be useful tools in understanding the psychological workings of organizations.

Until recent times, the norm in most U.S. organizations was certainly masculine—it still is in many organizations. A federal law enforcement agency and a telecommunications start-up come to mind as examples. In both cases, the predominant cultural values were "can-do" achievement and "whatever-it-takes" attention to the bottom line. We can now, however, point to some examples where the feminine is in the ascendence. In an all-female medical practice we are familiar with, the technical competence of the staff is high, while the dominant cultural feel is nurturing and healing. This gender *feel* of an organization has roots deep in the organization unconscious. Organizations with a masculine *feel* are probably tuned in primarily to the masculine energies of the Archetype of Organization, while those with a feminine *feel* probably resonate largely with the feminine energies of that archetype.

In his work with individuals, Jung emphasized the establishment of a gender identity as part of the work of the first half of life, and the development of the contrasexual complement (the anima, or unconscious feminine energies, in a man; the animus, or unconscious masculine energies, in a woman) as part of the task of maturation in midlife that balanced people out so that they could adequately shoulder the responsibilities of mature adult life. A start-up organization may have a relatively strong masculine or feminine identity and for a time be psychologically healthy. More developed organizations, however, may seem stunted and strangely adolescent if they do not achieve relative gender equilibrium. Signs of gender balance in an organization include:

> ‣ some relative balance of both sexes at all levels of the
> organization;

▶ both male and female employees feeling comfortable and appropriately secure in the organization; and

▶ both males and females in the loop with real decision making in the organization.

The absence of any of these three elements may suggest an imbalance of feminine and masculine energies.

Typology. The basic nature of an organization's center of consciousness can also be understood to some degree in terms of the typological functions and attitudes that characterize the individual ego. Jung posited that the ego could be described using a system that included two perceptive functions (*sensation* and *intuition*), two logical functions (*thinking* and *feeling*); and two attitudes (*extraversion* and *introversion*).[8] Isabel Myers later suggested that two additional attitudes (*Judging* and *Perceiving*) were also part of the mix, adding dimensions not explicitly identified in Jung's typology.[9] The four mental functions and four attitudes form a kind of intellectual compass that helps the center of consciousness orient the organization to both its external and internal realities. As with the individual ego, we find that one or two of the functions and two of the attitudes usually predominate in an organization's center of consciousness.[10]

William Bridges has taken the lead in using type concepts to further our understanding of organizations. He suggests, for example, that sensation and thinking characterize United Parcel Service as an organization, yielding an organizational character "focused on the actualities of the world rather than the possibilities."[11] In our experience, an organization's typelike characteristics can generally be inferred from the locus of attention of its center of consciousness. An organization's success depends upon having some access to all eight characteristics:

Introversion: The organization's center of consciousness is self-aware and capable of accurately assessing the organization's systems and habits.

Extraversion: The center of consciousness is aware of the external world, especially of market forces.

Sensing: The center of consciousness handles detail well and can easily face the facts of current realities.

Intuition: The center of consciousness sees the big picture, plans ahead, and is open to unexpected inspirations.

Thinking: The center of consciousness uses cause and effect analysis to think through problems.

Feeling: The center of consciousness is emotionally intelligent, attentive to human concerns, and able to use a-causal logic in its decision making.

Judging: The center of consciousness values orderliness and appropriate rules, and makes timely decisions.

Perceiving: The center of consciousness is open to new information and knows when to let a process take its course.

As with the individual ego, the center of consciousness tends to forget about or devalue the typelike functions and the attitude that it does not consciously prefer. These characteristics tend to get relegated to the organization's shadow, where they remain a resource waiting to be tapped.

PUBLIC FACE

An organization has a *public face* that is roughly analogous to Jung's concept of the individual's persona. Jung viewed the persona as a "complex system of relations between the individual and the environment, a kind of an archetypal mask that, on the one hand, helps the individual make a definite impression upon the world and, on the other hand, conceals the individual's true nature."[12] Some aspects of the persona are known to and directed by the ego. Others are unknown to the ego, which is to say that they are expressions of the unconscious.

An organization's public face has the properties of both a structure and a process. It is a web of energy, relationships, and ideas that functions at the psychological boundary between the organization and its environment. An organization's public face serves as a kind of filter through which information and energy flow out of the organizational psyche. It is an expression of the whole of the organizational psyche, conscious and unconscious.

The center of consciousness is, of course, fully aware of the conscious part of the organization's public face and carefully cultivates it to create a *brand identity*. Organizations find many ways to express their brand identities, including product names, annual reports, marketing strategies, lobbying activities, recruiting literature, press releases, public relations strategies, official histories, logos, slogans, relations with regulatory agencies, advertising programs, web-sites, charitable works/ contributions, relations with trade associations, and customer focus groups, to name just a few.

The conscious aspect of the public face, the brand identity, does two things for the organization. First, it transmits the organization's ideal image of itself. Think of the bank that touts itself as the *friendly neighbor down at*

HELPS PEOPLE	BRANDS	ARCHETYPE
Be wholesome, good, and safe	Ivory Soap Disney	Innocent
Feel free, expand horizons	Starbucks Levi's	Explorer
Understand their world	Oprah Winfrey MIT	Sage
Act courageously	Nike March of Dimes	Hero
Break the rules	Harley-Davidson Apple	Revolutionary
Affect transformation	MasterCard Calgon	Magician
Be O.K. just as they are	Wendy's Snapple	Everyperson
Find love and/or romance	Hallmark Victoria's Secret	Lover
Have a good time	Ben & Jerry's Miller Lite	Jester
Care for others	AT&T Campbell's Soups	Caregiver
Be artistic and creative	Martha Stewart Palm Pilot	Creator
Be responsible and prestigious	Day-Timer Lincoln	Ruler

the corner. Second, the public face screens from the operating environment aspects of the organization that the center of consciousness wants to hide. Underscoring this function is a recent newspaper report about a Maryland county government's concern that too many pawnshops were "damaging the county's public persona."[13]

The rest of the public face remains unknown to the center of consciousness, expressing various contents of the organization unconscious: the organization shadow and the various archetypal energies at work in the organizational psyche. For example, a church went out of its way to advertise itself as a place where *all* are welcome, while its location, the dress of its parishioners, and the kinds of cars they parked in the church parking lot broadcast an unintended, shadow message of exclusivity.

In the end, an organization's public face is a compromise between how the center of consciousness wants to present the organization and what the environment wants or expects of the organization. In seeking to find its niche, the organization inevitably caters to some degree to what its public wants. In so doing it may to a greater or lesser degree have to sublimate parts of itself. The sublimated material will end up in the organization's shadow.

The recent enthusiasm in organizations for "branding," not just products but the organizations themselves, makes the negotiation of a public face a more conscious effort than it once was; it also makes it a more profound enterprise. At best, branding is an exercise in connecting the organization's conscious life with its unconscious life and with the public. The brand identity emphasizes one of the archetypes most important to the organizational culture, one that is appropriate to the organization's major services, product lines, or messages and that will appeal to its customers, clients, or public.[14]

A healthy public face is by definition a useful one, helping the organization to make its way in the world. In the best case, the center of consciousness becomes sufficiently aware of its shadow stuff to minimize the chance that it will *leak* into the organization's public face. It uses that understanding to proceed with great humility and caution, knowing that there will always be aspects of the organization unconscious that remain unknown to the center of consciousness and which will be communicated autonomously to the environment. In the best case, the center of consciousness becomes aware of some of the archetypal energies stirring within the organization. It can use that understanding to shape a public face that reflects those energies with deep integrity and authenticity. In our experience, the most successful and useful public face always expresses some archetypal truth about the organization. Johnson & Johnson is a good example. The company's public relations strategy following the Tylenol scare reflected core organizational values carried by the archetypal energy of the Caregiver.[15]

MAPPING AN ORGANIZATION'S PSYCHE

We invite you now to continue using Jungian Organization Theory to map the psyche of an organization you know well and whose well-being matters to you. Turn to part two, answer the questions under task one/step three, and record your answers on the accompanying worksheet.

Notes

1. Jung (*C.W. 6*, para. 706).

2. The evolution of our thinking about the center of consciousness was influenced in part by Bion (1952, pp. 235–247), who made a case for the existence of a collective, egolike activity in groups; and by Abt (1988, p. 300), who asserts that the function of a city for its surrounding region is fully analogous to the function of human ego-consciousness for the psyche. The city, he argues, constitutes a "supraordinate center of a common sphere of experience." Our concept of the center of consciousness differs somewhat from the thinking of Auger and Arneberg (in Stein and Hollwitz, 1992, p. 41), who argue that the chief executive officer or manager of an organization functions as the organization's ego.

3. Rayner (1992).

4. Menninger (1975, p. 279).

5. Tyler (1997).

6. Petzinger (1997).

7. Jung (*C.W. 10*, para. 275).

8. For the basic description of the four functions, see Jung (*C.W. 6*, paras. 901–903). For Jung's hypothesis that both thinking and feeling are logical functions, see Jung (*C.W. 6*, para. 953). This material was useful in leading us to understand that we needed to conceptualize organizational typology as a function of an organization's center of consciousness.

9. Myers (1980).

10. Jung (*C.W. 6*, pp. xiv-xv and paras. 899–901).

11. Bridges (1992, pp. 1–5).

12. Jung (*C.W. 7*, paras. 305, 505); and Wilmer (1987, p. 65).

13. Meyer (1997).

14. See Mark and Pearson (2001) for a full exploration of brands and their connection to both conscious and unconscious organizational processes.

15. Mark and Pearson (2001, p. 345).

CHAPTER FOUR

Organizational
Psychodynamics:
Pitfalls

If all the elements of the organizational psyche are allowed to play their natural roles in a continual balancing and rebalancing of psychic energy— between consciousness and the unconscious, masculine and feminine, shadow and light—they can foster the fluid homeostasis that is the key to organizational health. But when the parts of the organizational psyche are not in dialogue, energy needed for healthy development and productive processes can all too easily be blocked or wasted. This psychological fragmenting cuts off the organization from itself, its head from its body, consciousness from the unconscious.

In this chapter, we will explore four primary zones of the organizational psyche where this "dis-membering" can happen. Think of them as four categories of pitfalls, if you will, where the blocked or misdirected energy can result in organizational errors and ineffectiveness, poor morale, low productivity, wasted time, stunted creativity, or the abuse and disaffection of organization members. But also put in the back of your mind the notion that they represent four sets of hints about the potential energy for productive changes in an organization's psyche. Taken together, these four zones provide the concerned observer with a framework for assessing the relative health of an organization's psyche, for forming hypotheses about why things are the way they are, and for zeroing in on the things that most need attention. The four zones are as follows:

Zone 1: The Organizational Boundary and Beyond

Zone 2: The Center of Consciousness

Zone 3: Organizational Complexes

Zone 4: The Cusp of the Collective Unconscious

FIGURE 6 *Organizational Psychodynamics: Pitfalls*

ZONE 1:
Problematic Public Face Projection

ZONE 2:
Problematic Center of Consciousness Repression & Denial

ZONE 3:
Problematic Complexes

ZONE 4:
Disconnection from Collective Unconsciousness

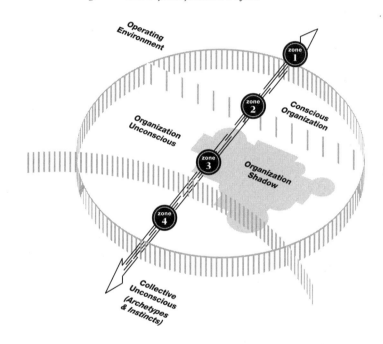

ZONE 1 PROBLEMS AT THE ORGANIZATIONAL BOUNDARY AND BEYOND

Difficulties in this zone of the Organizational Psyche can show up in a problematic public face or in organizational projection.

Problematic Public Face

Remember that the organization's public face is a web of ideas and energy at the boundary between the organization and its environment. It represents the organization's ideal image of itself; it also mediates between that image and the expectations the outer world has of the organization. Problems can arise when the public face is out of sync with the archetypal energies at work in the organization; when the public face unconsciously transmits material from the organization shadow; or when the center of consciousness comes to see the organization's public face as being the same thing as the organization.

Public Face Is out of Sync with Archetypal Energies. At Coca Cola, the decision to throw out its famous traditional formula and proceed with making *New Coke* was a marketing disaster.[1] In making this decision the company's center of consciousness seemed oblivious to the archetypal energy powering its flagship *Coke* brand. The powers failed to understand that, for its customers, the *Coke* brand tapped deeply into the yearning for normalcy and stability carried by the energy of the Innocent.[2] The decision to go with *New Coke* broke the company's archetypal connection with its customers. The powers also failed to see that the Innocent had come to play a core role in their own organization's culture. Going to *New Coke* put the organization in the position of selling a product that it did not really believe in—one that did not reflect the deep, archetypally mediated meaning of the organization.

Public Face Transmitting Shadow Material. At General Electric in the years before Jack Welch took over as chief executive officer, company lore had it that the company operated with its "face to the CEO and its rear end to the customer." Despite the usual public claims about how much GE valued its customers, many of the best managers were said to devote more energy to the care and feeding of the bureaucracy than to their customers' needs.[3] Here was a situation where the organization's public face emitted contradictory signals. The center of consciousness was purposefully signaling that the organization valued its customers, while at the same time the behavior of some managers was signaling a shadow-based contempt for those same customers.

Public Face Seen as Being Same Thing as the Organization. In one large bureaucratic organization the center of consciousness insisted in its recruiting activities that the organization easily and routinely attracted the *best and the brightest,* and in fact had always done so. The reality, as seen by many organization members, as well as by knowledgeable outsiders, was that the organization attracted and retained a few stars, but that the rest of the employee population was pretty average. The center of consciousness in this case seems to have confused the image it was trying to project with an inner reality about which it was oblivious, or chose to ignore.

Organizational Projection

Organizational projection is an unconscious psychological process in which the center of consciousness experiences an intense emotional reaction to a quality or attitude it *sees* in another entity, when in fact the quality or attitude is a content of the projecting organization's own unconscious. Organizational projection is a natural and autonomous act. An organization does not consciously or willfully project, so much as encounter the projections of itself in partners or other entities. The problem is not that an organization projects. In fact, a projection recognized and analyzed can be an important vehicle for heightening an organization's awareness of itself. The problem lies in the lack of awareness. Unrecognized or unacknowledged projection can rob energy from the necessary dialog between the center of consciousness and the organization unconscious.

An organization will routinely project any and all of the contents of its unconscious onto other entities.[4] Here are several examples. In our fable, the Bramblebush—a stand-in here for the partnership—seems to be engaging in a kind of projective activity as it *reaches out* to pluck at the garments of passersby to see if any of the cloth is really his. A women's college one of us worked with projected its own repressed masculine energy onto coeducational colleges, thereby greatly exaggerating in its collective mind the sexism of those colleges. The result was an inability on the part of the school's administration to understand why so few young women were choosing women's colleges over co-educational ones. A government agency that one of us has worked with for years accused *another* agency of being untrustworthy and uncooperative—failing to recognize that its own behaviors toward the other epitomized untrustworthiness and uncooperativeness. Across the United States, managed health organizations and physician groups accuse each other of being "in it" only for the money—each side is unwilling to accept this as one of its own motives. Another company envies the commitment of a competitor to corporate learning. In its envying, it is simply *seeing* its own hidden-from-view ability to make the same commitment. It is in effect projecting its own embodiment of the Archetype of Organization onto the other organization.[5] Finally, organizations can project their complexes onto entities outside the organization. (For more on this, see the discussion of complexes later in this chapter.)

An organization can also project unconscious material inwardly onto groups of its own members. An organization that has a tightly drawn list of *acceptable* attitudes and behaviors has essentially repressed *otherness* or *different from* us in its unconscious. If the center of consciousness does not acknowledge the repression, it will be prone to projecting this repressed energy onto those organization members who embody the difference—and often unconsciously sustaining policies that discriminate against those who are different. This dynamic has negatively affected people of color and women in many organizations for many years. Widespread diversity interventions have begun to raise its harmfulness to consciousness.

ZONE 2 PROBLEMS AT THE CENTER OF CONSCIOUSNESS
Difficulties in this zone of the Organizational Psyche can show in a problematic center of consciousness or in the dynamic of repression and denial.

Problematic Center of Consciousness

Since the center of consciousness governs what information is allowed into the decision-making process, issues here may mean that an organization is not always able to track all the information that it needs to notice in order to be effective. A Jungian approach to understanding organizational dynamics widens the range of what managerial leaders must pay attention to. The strength of the center of consciousness determines whether appropriate action can be taken on what is known. The center of consciousness can be troublesome in one of three ways: it may simply be weak; it may be embodied in too few people; or it may have developed in a one-sided fashion, i.e., unbalanced with respect to the four basic energies of the Archetype of Organization.

Weak. A not-for-profit organization one of us has worked with had what we would describe as a weak center of consciousness. The director—in effect a one-person center of consciousness—could neither articulate an overall sense of direction for the organization nor align the various departmental leaders and their employees to support a larger purpose. As a result, each department went its own way, often competing with others for clients and resources. At least one department always seemed to be in crisis. As the organization teetered on the brink of disaster, the board of directors ineffectually tried to impose order from the outside. A second example of an underdeveloped center of consciousness is a human resource department in a large government organization. The department's motto was: "We're from HR . . . how can we help?" On the face of it, that seems like a reasonable stance to take, but it led to a dynamic in which the HR department could never say no—it had no boundary. As it attempted to do things for which it was not equipped, the department experienced many failures and found itself in one situation after another where it was mocked and scapegoated by the larger organization.

Embodied in Too Few. Equally problematic can be a center of consciousness that is strong enough but embodied in too few people. When an organization's operating environment is relatively stable and unchanging, a tightly circumscribed center of consciousness, i.e., one invested in relatively few people, may be able to lead an organization quite effectively. However, when an operating environment becomes unstable and unpredictable, an organization that tries to manage with a tightly circumscribed center of consciousness is at risk of trying to deal with exponentially increasing complexity with too few brains engaged in helping it adapt. This situation faced many organizations in the 1980s and 1990s. General Electric may be emblematic of the lot. In 1981, Jack Welch took over a company that he thought was about to take a bad fall because its highly centralized and bureaucratized decision-making structure was inadequate to the task of leading GE through the far-reaching changes he saw lying ahead. Welch had to deal with a management culture that liked workers to "park their brains at the door each day before they started to work."[6] Implicitly, he seems to have understood that GE's center of consciousness was too narrowly drawn.

Unbalanced. The center of consciousness can also be a source of problems for an organization when its attitudes and actions do not reflect all of the basic impulses embedded in the Archetype of Organization. People Express, the now-defunct, low-cost airline, is a case in point. At People Express, the founding myth—values/vision—celebrated innovation and people.[7] During the company's short life, the company's center of consciousness was passionate about meeting its customers' needs, creating and implementing new ideas, and treating its employees well. The company got off the ground quickly and enjoyed several years in which success piled on top of success. The company, spurred by the *Learning* energy of the Archetype of Organization, became synonymous with innovation in the airline industry.[8] At the same time, it ignored the need to build adequate management and financial systems, neglecting, we would suggest, the *Stabilizing* impulses in the Archetype of Organization. People Express was sold in its fifth year to rival Texas Air.

The experiences of recent years of two now defunct colleges also point to the dangers of one-sidedness. At Trinity of Vermont, the culture was supportive, collegial, and inward-looking. The *People* energy of the Archetype of Organization, particularly the Lover aspect, predominated. As one faculty member put it, "the college loved itself to death," as it missed one opportunity after another to move and grow with its environment until it was too late. In Mt. Vernon College's early years, the college was a haven for wealthy young girls. Any budget shortfall was solved by one wealthy patron, who simply pulled out a check book; this bred an Innocent culture that expected rescue. The college's attachment to keeping everything the way it was in the *good old* days—the down-side of Innocent energy—made people resistant to responding to a changing admissions reality until the situation was too dire to be salvaged.

We should note here that there may be times in the life of an organization when a lop-sided center of consciousness, i.e., one that does not reflect all four dimensions of the Archetype of Organization may be inevitable, perhaps for a time even fairly robust. The formative years of an organization may be such a time, although this is not necessarily true of all start-ups. In this period of organizational life it could be entirely appropriate for the organization's energy to be focused on *doing whatever it takes* to ensure that the organization will survive.

A start-up organization must focus narrowly on differentiating itself from other organizations and convincing the marketplace that it offers something of value. Like the ego in the youthful individual, the center of consciousness in a young organization accomplishes this differentiation by making a great number of rapid-fire, either/or choices about how it will do its business—always against the backdrop of needing those choices to support *making it.* And for an organization this typically means that in the early years, the full diversity of views and values inherent in the Archetype of Organization may not come to the fore. This can be seen in Bill Gates's tendency during Microsoft's early years to hire largely in his own image: young, white, males—who took *flak* from no one, churned out computer code in frenzied bursts, drove their cars fast, and had the kind of no-limits mentality that Gates saw in himself.[9]

▸ ▸ ▸

Organizational Life Stages

The organizational psyche model provides a framework for tracking an organization's developmental journey from birth to maturity, and perhaps even death. Like people, organizations may be seen as experiencing three major life phases. Like people, organizations may experience each of these phases more than once or may experience them in any order. Other organizations may move through the phases in such a nondramatic way as to make them barely discernible.

In phase one, an organization's formative and early years—or the new beginnings occasioned by a merger or take-over—an organization will be focused necessarily on adapting to the operating environment, doing whatever it takes to establish a niche for itself and survive. The energy flow within the organizational psyche will be from the center of consciousness out and through the various facets of the organization's public face. The overall character of the organization during this phase will be *collective-pleasing.* The organization's inner needs (and those of its employees) are likely to be less apparent and get less attention because most employees will be caught up in the energy of the founding vision and be closely aligned with it—even to the extent of sublimating some of their own critical personal wholeness needs. The organization unconscious and the collective unconscious will probably play a relatively small part in the organization's psychodynamics in this phase of the organizational life cycle. A single archetypal energy is often dominant in this phase, giving an organization an unbalanced culture.

In phase two, a period often marked by transition and crisis, an organization may find that the years of adapting to the operating environment and ignoring the inner needs of the organization and its members have taken their toll on creativity and adaptability; that the organization's products and services no longer seem to be meeting the customer's needs; that approaches, processes, and attitudes which served the center of consciousness and the organization well during the organization's early years no longer work; and that energy levels and morale are in decline. The primary flow of psychic energy will be confused and unfocused. Remnants of the outward flow may be intact, but the autonomous voice of the organization unconscious and the collective unconscious may start calling the organization to look within.

The center of consciousness needs to do something. But what? The question is a difficult one, because both the problem facing the organization and the solution lie largely at the feet of the center of consciousness. In the typical organization, the center of consciousness gets to organizational midlife having utilized a relatively small percentage of the possibilities of organization—the values, norms, approaches, biases, and methods that make up the universe of organizational behavior as embodied in the Archetype of Organization. Half of the possibilities that the center of consciousness encountered along the way were necessarily repressed into the organization unconscious as it forged a coherent organizational stance to deal with the do-or-die mission and task demands of the early years. Another set of possibilities lies in the organization unconscious and in the collective unconscious—possibilities completely outside the organization's conscious experience to date.

For such organizations, the choice is between staying on the same old path with its risks of stagnation or choosing the discomfort and uncertainty of starting to explore the unconscious unknown, with its promise of new possibilities and new productive energies, and undertaking a serious, intentional dialogue with the organization unconscious and the collective unconscious.

In phase three, the period of psychological maturity, an organization will begin to move toward its full and unique manifestation of the Archetype of Organization. The primary flow of psychic energy will be between the center of consciousness and the collective unconscious, mediated by the Archetype of Organization.[10]

▸ ▸ ▸

Doing whatever it takes to survive may be inevitable, but in our experience it seldom works as a long-term strategy. While the center of consciousness lives out those parts of the Archetype of Organization that help the organization survive, other aspects of this central archetype either remain unknown to the center of consciousness or are repressed into the organization shadow. In the case of Microsoft, the energies of *Learning* and *Results* were dominant in the early days, while the *People* and *Stabilizing* impulses remained hidden in the budding organization's unconscious. We believe that most organizations, even the Microsofts of the world, eventually run up against the limits of one-sidedness: in the absence of adequate balance, the center of consciousness can become enthralled by the controlling archetypal forces with negative results (e.g., an antitrust case).

Repression and Denial

As an organization grows and develops, it naturally and inevitably represses into the organization shadow an agglomeration of contents, such as thoughts, feelings, and behaviors that do not fit *the way we do things here*; skeletons of various kinds; stories about failures and scapegoats; nonpreferred *typological* functions; and various "isms." Some of the contents of the shadow have an unambiguously negative valence and deserve to stay forever consciously disconnected from the organization's day-to-day activities. Clearly unethical and antisocial attitudes and behaviors might be examples of this. Other contents of an organization's shadow, however, will have been repressed more or less arbitrarily by the center of consciousness and represent potential energy for growth and renewal. The repression of the feminine principle noted previously would fall into this category.

Problems arise in this zone of the organizational psyche primarily when the center of consciousness denies the reality of the shadow and fails to examine its contents as an organization grows and changes. Unfortunately, the bias for rationality and *scientific management* that governs managerial behavior in many organizations tends to encourage this kind of denial on the part of the center of consciousness in many organizations. This bias can make it unacceptable and risky for organization members to talk about shadow material, let alone work with it.

We offer three examples where the repression/denial dynamic has caused problems. The first example is the partnership in our fable. Here is an organization that has repressed into its shadow the capacity it once had for creatively engaging its customers and creditors. Its members deny the organization's previous competence and engage in a variety of pointless and ineffectual activities. There is gold in this organization's shadow that it needs to redeem if it is to return to health.

The second example is a large department of a government agency. In this organization, the thinking function dominated the activities carried out by the center of consciousness. Causal logic, objectivity, and hard facts were the coins of the realm. Organization members who attempted to bring a-causal connectivity, subjectivity, or emotions—the currencies of the feeling function—into business discussions were ridiculed and their contributions ignored. The feeling function was repressed into the organization's shadow, and the possibility that it could add value was never considered.

The third example is a nongovernmental agency. There was fairly clear evidence of institutional racism in its internal operations. Despite talk to the contrary by those embodying the center of consciousness, the organization had in effect repressed racial equality and equal opportunity into its shadow. The center of consciousness feared examining the issue of institutional racism and avoided doing so. This prevented the organization from moving with choice, with forgiveness and energy, to establish policies and procedures that could lead to fundamental change.

Until the center of consciousness recognizes and to some degree integrates the shadow into conscious organizational processes, an organization will remain psychologically immature. It will also deny itself the opportunity to experience a great rush of generativity and originality. By recognizing and coming to grips with the contents of the organization shadow, organizations can tap new sources of creativity and become much more humane, vibrant, and morally responsive and responsible.[11]

ZONE 3 PROBLEMS WITH ORGANIZATIONAL COMPLEXES

As with the individual complex, the organizational complex is a natural part of an organization's psychic landscape. It is problematic only when it becomes overly energized by emotion and affect and/or when the negative (demonic) qualities of the archetypal core of the complex come to the fore. At this point, the complex overwhelms normal organizational functioning. It is as though the center of consciousness enters into a trancelike, primitive state in which it loses its capacity to operate in productive and creative ways. It is in a sense possessed. In its overheated, problematic state, an organizational complex can—as long as it remains unconscious—manifest itself in several dysfunctional and often inter-related ways, including "identity," "compulsiveness," "projection," and "inflation."[12]

Identity. The organization becomes the complex. We have both worked with organizations where Total Quality Management has been practiced with near religious fervor. Under this prescription for organizational improvement, the customer is deemed the only measure of organizational effectiveness. Literally no other criteria have any validity. No credence is given to the possibility that the customer may in fact be wrong and in need of help to determine what is needed. This stance is heatedly defended. There has ceased to be a psychological boundary between the center of consciousness and the customer. These organizations could be said to have negative customer complex. An organization that lives by the motto *the customer is always right* may be possessed by the demonic energy of the Innocent or Caregiver. It has set itself up for victimization, inasmuch as this stance is overly accommodating and robs the organization of the ability to push back appropriately when a customer needs help being right or when a customer's demand runs counter to a legitimate but conflicting need of the organization itself.

Compulsiveness. The organization is driven. At General Electric,

As If and Its Consequences

When caught in any of the pitfalls under discussion here, an organization will find itself operating in *as if* mode. In the midst of projection, the center of consciousness behaves *as if* the qualities—negative or positive—it sees in other entities actually belong to the other. In the state of denial, the center of consciousness functions *as if* the organization's unconscious parts were not real. In the grip of an over-loaded complex, the center of consciousness operates *as if* it is in charge, when in fact the complex is running the show. Ignoring the collective unconscious, the center of consciousness operates as if the managers really can control everything.

prior to the arrival of Jack Welch, there was a five-volume set of manuals known as the *Blue Books*. Taken together, these five volumes prescribed how to manage GE in minute detail. Although GE managers moved frequently, they could turn to the *Blue Books* for advice on what to do in virtually any situation.[13] This scenario suggests compulsiveness on the part of the center of consciousness, trying in vain to take the risk out of organizational life and cover every contingency. It suggests the existence of a problematic *control complex* that rendered managers and employees childlike and sapped the organization's ability to adapt to a changing environment. This control complex was probably energized in part by the dark side of the Ruler, which can infect organizational problem-solving with the illusion of control—a learning disability often found in organizations where power and authority are the main political currencies.

Projection. The organization projects the complex onto another entity. Caught in the use of child labor in China, Nike reneged on gifts promised to universities that supported student-led efforts to impose standards for the protection of the international labor force. The firm's policy had tarnished its reputation.[14] With this action, Nike in essence said, "We aren't the problem, you are." Nike continued to see itself as the good guy, while virtually everyone else saw it as the villain, suggesting that Nike had projected a negatively charged *survival complex*. This complex probably owed some of its force to the demonic side of the Hero, which can engender a siege mentality and a tendency to see the world through an *us versus them* lens.

Inflation. The organization becomes overly filled with itself. Months of high energy, closed-door sessions working toward a major organizational restructuring left the center of consciousness in a large company convinced that it had hit upon a perfect solution to the organization's problems. The plan was unveiled with much ceremony and self-congratulation. A major communication campaign was set in motion to explain the change and get employees to "buy in." But employees saw the plan as rearranging deck chairs on the *Titanic,* and customers and stakeholders were indifferent. Moreover, a consultant called in to help implement the restructuring suggested that the plan had actually overlooked several major issues. An over-energized mastery complex had robbed the center of consciousness of the ability to see the situation objectively and get the necessary input from other sources. Such a complex was likely fed by the dark energy of the Sage, which can imprison the center of consciousness in the proverbial ivory tower, disconnecting it from reality.

As the foregoing examples suggest, an organizational complex is to a significant degree autonomous. When an organization is caught up in an

Organizations in *as if* mode will often exhibit one or more of these characteristics: passivity/low energy, circularity of discussion, lack of real progress, *us-versus-them* language, organizational irritability, denigration of the task/problem, and resistance to reflecting on the process. In general, an organization operating in one of these *as if* modes will find itself *unable* to do things despite the fact that it has every skill and ability it needs to undertake them.

Maintaining the alternative reality implied by these *as if* conditions requires an immense amount of an organization's limited psychic energy. It amounts, in effect, to channeling large quantities of the organization's libido away from its natural, productive course and into a psychic black hole of pretend behavior—never a healthy position for an organization to be in—and few organizations can afford such waste in an era of tight resources.

over-energized or negatively charged complex, the complex *has* the organization, not the other way around. It is as though the Archetype of Organization loses its ability to channel and balance the archetypal energies flowing into the organization, and the psychological life of the organization becomes dangerously one-sided. Organizational dysfunction results. Unable to deal with problematic complexes and the potentially explosive conflicts they engender, organizations all too often resort to "exporting their problems through firings, splits, and other structural changes that hide the real psychodynamic processes at work."[15]

The exportation of complex-related problems becomes all too evident in the contemporary context of mergers and acquisitions. If the dominant party to the merger has problematic complexes, they are often projected onto the less dominant party involved, creating a "my way or the highway" mentality that justifies a gobbling up of the *lesser* entity *as if* there were no value whatsoever in its approaches to work or its organizational culture. The people in the acquired group feel as if their reality is being denied and negated. The field of feelings is similar to that in the colonization process. The colonizing nation cloaks its efforts in assertions that it is trying to *help* the colony, *civilize* it, and help it do things *right*. This is not, however, how the colonized culture generally experiences the result. The people in the colonized culture are more likely to characterize the process as destroying everything they hold dear.

ZONE 4 PROBLEMS ON THE CUSP
OF THE COLLECTIVE UNCONSCIOUS

Nearly all of the organizations we know anything about base their operations firmly on the principles of scientific management. In many of these organizations, there is barely a suspicion that there might be any limits on rationality or on the ability of ego-directed action to solve all problems.[16] This, despite no end of *as if* behavior suggesting the working of various unconscious forces. In the rest, there may or may not be some awareness that rationality has limits, but in one way or another these organizations have bumped up against or stumbled into archetypal territory at some point, and the experience has generated a deep fear of examining the consequences of this fact.

One example of the first group would be any number of organizations caught up in downsizing. Our experience is that when organizations are laying off people, deep archetypal energies relating to abandonment, death, and loss abound. Typically in these organizations, however, the center of consciousness tries to act as if there are no deep feelings about the people getting axed and that business can proceed as usual.

General Electric seems to be another example of the first group. Jack Welch by most measures did a fabulous job at GE, transforming the company's business, its work processes, and in some significant ways its very culture. But he showed one blind spot that limited his impact in an arena that by his own acknowledgment was quite important. During his tenure, Welch focused on engaging the mind of every employee.[17] And, by all accounts, he had considerable success in this regard. He also made clear, however, that he wanted GE to become a place where "a sense of accomplishment is rewarded in . . . the [employee's] soul."[18] But there is little if any evidence that he ever put in place a process for dealing with the *soul* issues. This would have meant connecting with the employees' psyches and the psyche of the organization as a whole. For that work, a continuing focus on conscious processes and activities would not suffice. He stopped well short of any acknowledgment that there might be irrational (i.e., unconscious) dimensions to life at GE or that dealing with those aspects might require an admission of limits on the sway of rational managerial action.

A government organization one of us worked with appears to be one example of the second group. The organization was sunk deep in apathy and lack of clarity about its mission. All manner of conventional change processes had been tried to no avail. The consultant recommended trying Open Space Technology, an intervention in which organization members are invited to come together to talk about an organizational issue in a *retreat* setting governed by self-identified and self-organized groups.[19] After the consultant explained this technique and the fact that it often has the effect of summoning up archetypal energies and imagery from the participants, the client demurred, arguing that the organization's problems were clear enough and that the change tools that had been tried simply hadn't been used effectively. The client's solution was to let things sit for awhile and see what happened. That may have been the right call, but we suspect that the description of the Open Space Technology intervention, though in some ways attractive to the client, sounded ephemeral, almost mystical and raised fears in the client's eyes of being out of control—out of ego control, that is. Somehow, the client seems to have had a sense that once out the genie would not fit back into the bottle.

Another example of the second group are the many organizations that have engaged in visioning processes that unwittingly connect with unconscious energies. Energized by archetypal forces, the product of the visioning efforts can often be frightening to the center of consciousness, and the ideas generated are all too often put on the shelf. People who invested in the process can then become dispirited and disillusioned, checking out of real involvement in any such enterprises in the future.

Ultimately, an organization's movement toward *organizational whole-ness* requires a dramatic change in the relationships between the center of consciousness and the unconscious realm of the organization. The center of consciousness must come to recognize that the Archetype of Organization has an autonomous and useful perspective on the life of the organization. Only then can the balancing of conscious and unconscious energies provide the organization the sense of both stability and dynamism it needs to function in a healthy way. The center of consciousness that is unaware of or fearful of dealing with the realm of the archetypes is likely to stick with the comfort and certainty of the possibilities it knows. Like the middle-aged man who buys a flashy car and courts a younger woman in the mistaken belief that he can recapture his youth, the organization in denial of the need to grow up may try to maintain the organization's vital-ity by *getting back to basics,* trying to *do more with less,* or chasing the latest management fad. Such approaches may yield some positives for a time— profits might pick up and energy levels in the organization might even rise. But this stance risks depriving an organization of a vast font of energy and insight that few organizations can afford to neglect.

MAPPING AN ORGANIZATION'S PSYCHE

Continue, now, the process of using Jungian Organization Theory to map the psyche of an organization you know well and whose well-being matters to you. Turn to part two, answer the questions under task two, and record your answers on the accompanying worksheet.

Notes

1. Tyler (1997).

2. Mark and Pearson (2001, p. 60).

3. Tichy and Sherman (1993, pp. 6, 33,157).

4. Marshak and Katz (1990, pp. 58-59) appear to embrace this idea when they write that the organization unconscious manifests itself in organizational projections, stereotyping, and compensatory behaviors.

5. Stein (in Stein and Hollwitz, 1992, p. 8).

6. Slater (1993, p. 210).

7. Quinn (1988, pp 72–76).

8. Ibid.

9. Manes and Andrews (1993, pp. 104,196).

10. Various writers-among them Stein (1983); Whitmont (1969, p. 139); Edinger (1972, pp. 37, 87, 160, 261); Pearson (1991); and Jacobi (1965, p. 38)—have suggested that the life of the individual consists of three phases: an *ego* phase, in which the emphasis is on accommodating to the external world; a *transitional* phase, in which an individual's

energies begin shifting away from the world; and an *individuating* phase in which the self becomes more assertive, and healthy development requires that the ego give way to the task of inner development toward the unique image of wholeness stored in the self. Pearson describes these stages as an ego-oriented preparation phase, a soul-focused journey or transition phase, and an integrated self-connected return phase. This set of ideas was helpful to us in conceptualizing the diachronic development of organizations.

11. Morgan (1986, p. 225).

12. Whitmont (1969, p. 58) discusses these dynamics in the individual psyche. Jacobi (1959, p. x) was an influence on the development of our ideas about normal and problematic complexes in organizations.

13. Tichy and Sherman (1993, pp. 27, 34,37) and Slater (1993, p. 25).

14. Mark and Pearson (2001, p. 110).

15. Colman (in Stein and Hollwitz,1992, p. 114).

16. Corlett (2000).

17. Swoboda (1997).

18. Tichy and Charan (1989).

19. Owen (1992).

CHAPTER FIVE

Organizational Psychodynamics: Pathways

Helping organizations escape from the black hole of *as if* dynamics or helping them understand and engage the positive stirrings of archetypal energy deep within is important and challenging work. And there are abundant opportunities for assisting organizations in re-membering themselves in each of the four zones of the organizational psyche we discussed in chapter 4. In this chapter we will first consider whole-making processes in general and then examine in some detail approaches to whole-making that are best suited for each of the four zones.

WHOLE-MAKING: *RE-MEMBERING* THE ORGANIZATION

Organizational whole-making focuses on getting and keeping the energy flowing along the psychological axis running from the collective unconscious, through the Archetype of Organization and the center of consciousness, and on to the organization's center of consciousness and public face. Organizational whole-making is never completed, and the overall quality of such efforts is like peering through a fogged-up window inasmuch as we can only see and analyze the signs, traces, and indirect manifestations of the organization unconscious. As with individuals, awareness of the unconscious for most organizations comes only in bits and pieces. The unconscious is a bottomless well.

Organizational whole-making is a set of interrelated processes aimed at the following:

- healing those organizational troubles with their roots in unhealthy unconscious dynamics;
- aligning the conscious organization with the unconscious blueprint of organization stored in the Archetype of Organization; and
- tapping into the energy of the collective unconscious and the archetypes generally.

Whole-making interventions all have elements of analysis, assessment, action, and change; and they all contribute to both healing and transformation.

Whole-making processes operate in a framework of growth. Jung-grounded organizational work must start by suspending Chronos—human-reckoned time—and its rules (efficiency and linearity) and by creating a container defined by Kairos—in those days, once upon a time, a time out of time—and its rules (wholeness, creativity, and generativity). In this approach to helping organizations, development and change are understood to be holistic, synchronistic, and transformational—the result of the union of consciousness and the unconscious.

The approach to understanding the organizational psyche we have proposed in this book helps put the process of delving into organization unconscious into perspective. In the end, it is not the organization unconscious and its contents that are central; they are only important insofar as they provide balance and compensation to the larger organizational processes. Plumbing the organization's unconscious is not enough. In fact, by itself such digging can be irrelevant at best and dangerous at worst. Although the organization unconscious contains all manner of shadow and archetypal material with the potential for fostering greater organizational health, this potential can only be actualized if the center of consciousness engages it, analyzes it, and carries it over from Kairos into Chronos and the realm of conscious organizational processes.

PATHWAYS TO WHOLENESS

All whole-making activities are intended to "move the organization toward consciousness, toward differentiation and improved communication, and toward greater tolerance."[1] And there is no particular order in which they must occur. The choice of whole-making activities may be ego-directed, orchestrated by the center of consciousness and/or a consultant to prevent a problem or explore a perceived opportunity. Just as likely, however, the need for whole-making activities may be dictated by the autonomous unconscious forces at work in the organization: a complex may flare up, requiring psychodynamic first aid; or the one-sidedness of the organization's conscious processes may trigger the expression of counter-balancing archetypal energy, offering the center of consciousness an opportunity to move the organizational psyche toward wholeness.

Regardless of how the need for work comes to the fore, the task of bringing about the desired interplay between organizational consciousness on the one hand and the organization unconscious and the collective unconscious on the other has two primary focuses. First, there must be clear and open communication between the center of consciousness and the organization unconscious. We have designated the locus of this dynamic as Zones 1 through 3 of the organizational psyche. Second, the center of consciousness must be open to information from the collective unconscious. We have designated the locus of this flow of energy as Zone 4 of the organizational psyche.

Zones 1 through 3. Whole-making in these arenas is carried out primarily through "processes of understanding."[2] In processes of under-

FIGURE 7 *Organizational Psychodynamics: Pathways*

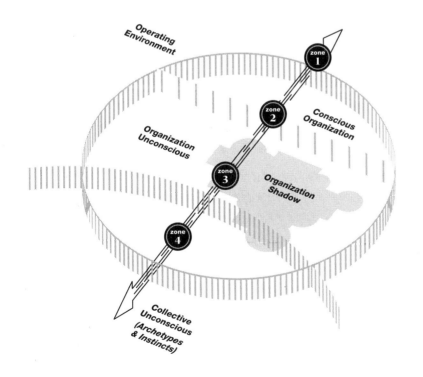

ZONE 1:
Strengthening Public Face Withdrawing Projections

ZONE 2:
Bolstering Center of Consciousness Owning the Shadow

ZONE 3:
De-energizing Complexes

ZONE 4:
Dialogue with the Collective Unconsciousness

standing, representatives of the center of consciousness—and in some cases other organization members and individuals from outside the organization—are invited to engage their intellects directly in gathering data about, assessing, and changing the organization's psychodynamic processes for the better. These approaches use concepts, frameworks, and models; experiential learning techniques; various analytical processes; and didactic presentations to convert energy trapped in an organization's *as if* behavior into knowledge the organization can use for its development. An example would be identifying and analyzing an organizational complex. Processes of understanding seek, in a sense, to increase the organization's emotional intelligence. They do not move the center of consciousness too far from its comfort zone, i.e., feeling that things are *under control*.

They can be thought of as housecleaning—getting the skeletons out of the closets, sorting out the contents of the attic—in preparation for the arrival of the invited guest: the archetypes and the collective unconscious.

In Zone 1, At the Organizational Boundary and Beyond, whole-making work focuses chiefly on making the organization's public face more vital and on identifying and withdrawing organizational projections.

Public Face. Developing a strong, flexible public face allows the organization to stand in a healthy give-and-take relationship with its environment, both shaping it and being shaped by it.

If the conscious, brand identity dimension of an organization's public face has gone *flat*—recall Coca Cola's near disaster with *New Coke,* it can be productive to intentionally *mine* the archetypal energies of the brand. Typically organizations blunder into and out of awareness of these archetypal energies. Mark and Pearson have laid out a more systematic approach to identifying the archetypal energies inherent in a brand identity and consciously cultivating the connections in the marketing of an organization's products and services. In examining many successful brands, they have found that the archetypal energies powering the brand are also at work in the cultures of the companies marketing the brands. Apple is an example.

Revolutionary energy—in its iconoclastic, "think different" guise— powers the Apple brand. It also informs the organization's *noncorporation* corporate culture. When Apple's board of directors tried to replace founder Steve Jobs with a more conventional manager, both employee morale and sales suffered. Only bringing back the trendsetting Jobs assuaged employee concerns and rekindled Apple's traditional customer fanaticism.[3] When Mark and Pearson's approach is followed, the branding process aligns the public identity of an organization with its deeper core truths.

If an organization's public face no longer supports the organization's day-to-day practices and processes, dealing with the situation using typological concepts can be fruitful. A company that grew from nothing as a manufacturer of medical equipment found that changing markets required it to provide consulting services to complement the equipment. Subjected to a *type* analysis, its original public face, characterized by *introverted thinking,* turned out to be a poor fit with a business model that required a strong dose of *extraverted feeling.* Armed with this insight, the company was in a position to alter its public stance toward its customer base.

Microsoft is an example of an organization where the center of consciousness faced up to a suddenly inadequate public face and created a new one. In its early years, Microsoft became synonymous in the computer software industry with technological innovation and youthful organizational informality. The center of consciousness put high stock in this way of doing business and the public image that went with it. But faced with the happy pains of skyrocketing growth, the organization's leadership came to recognize that the organization's continued success over the long run depended on its ability to marry its innovation and technical prowess with sober-minded business practices.[4] The center of consciousness, in other words, reevaluated its public face—to be sure, along with other aspects of the organization—and concluded that the old would no longer do. The center of consciousness proceeded to fashion a new public face that retained aspects of youthful insouciance but added new, more sober, businesslike facets better suited to the multimillion dollar giant Microsoft was becoming. In terms of the organization's typelike basic nature, this change could be described as balancing the strong *extraverted sensation* character of the youthful company with some *introverted thinking.*

Projection. If organizational projection is the problem—we noted previously the projective interplay between physicians' organizations and HMOs—it can be useful to engage a group representing the center of consciousness of the projecting organization in a conversation with a group of independent observers. To organize for the dialogue, ask each group to prepare privately on flip-chart paper the answers to the question: What do we say about the other organization?

Bring the groups together and facilitate a conversation between them designed to compare and contrast the lists. This approach can help members of the projecting organization recognize that its assertions about the other organization are idiosyncratic, help it embrace the *pogo dictum*— "We have met the enemy and it is us"—and withdraw the projection. Recognizing and withdrawing projections can lead to greater organizational maturity and heightened awareness by the center of consciousness of the organization's innate capabilities.

Data are often the best antidote to organizational projection. Recall the women's college that was projecting its own masculine energy onto coeducational colleges. All that was required to align the college's sense of reality with that of its market (and withdraw the projection) was a marketing study which made clear that eighteen-year-old women tended to prefer coeducational schools and to identify women's colleges with images of prim, maiden aunts.

If the center of consciousness has identified a person or group in the organization as the repository of the organization's problems, work with representatives of the center of consciousness to understand this as an unconscious projective process called "organizational scapegoating" that is deeply harmful to the person or group involved and that prevents the center of consciousness from addressing the underlying organizational deficiencies.[5]

In Zone 2, Working with the Center of Consciousness, whole-making work focuses chiefly on strengthening the center of consciousness and on helping it deal with material repressed into the organization shadow.

Bolstering the center of consciousness. If the initial assessment indicates a weak center of consciousness, we have found it productive to help representatives of the center of consciousness identify the typological character of the center of consciousness. Start by helping those involved understand their individual typologies. Then, work with and refine the hypothesis that the basic nature of the center of consciousness might be the modal type of the organization members who comprise the center of consciousness. It can also be useful to explore the possibility that this modal type reflects the preferences of the organization's founder and/or the organization's field of endeavor. Such analysis can provide the center of consciousness insights into the way it does business and set the stage for development of the nonpreferred characteristics.

If the center of consciousness is embodied in too few people—this seems to have been the case at the North Berwick, Maine, Pratt & Whitney plant, where the traditional management structure was having a difficult time keeping up with the pace of change—a profit-sharing program can motivate employees to take significantly more responsibility for product quality and cost cutting. After the Pratt and Whitney plant had moved in this direction, a manager in the plant noted: "We've got 1,500 people looking at what [a much smaller number of] managers used to look at."[6] We previously cited Jack Welch's concern that too few GE employees felt responsibility for the fate of GE.[7] To counter this he worked with consultants to utilize the Work-Out intervention throughout the organization. This process aimed at giving every GE employee the opportunity to offer ideas for organizational improvement, and then to hold the center of consciousness accountable for acting on the ideas raised.

If the center of consciousness has developed in an unhealthily one-sided manner—we previously cited People Express as an example—we suggest using either the *System Stewardship Survey*™ (appendix B) or the *Archetypal Leadership Styles Survey*™ (appendix C). Both the *Stewardship Survey*™ and the *Leadership Survey*™ can help the center of consciousness look at the deeply held sets of values and archetypal energies that underlie its behavior, to look at the impact of these values on the organization, and to consider the possible validity and utility of other sets of values. Invite representatives of the center of consciousness to fill out the two surveys. Amalgamate the individual scores to create a rough organizational profile. Identify and discuss patterns that can lead to greater collective awareness of the need for adding dimensions not evident in the profile to the way the center of consciousness goes about its business.

Denial and Repression. For problems associated with the denial of repressed material, try gathering data from organization members who embody thoughts, feelings, behaviors, and characteristics that the organization has repressed. Diversity panels—often representing organization members whose values and behaviors have been disregarded by an organization—can be a rich source of information in this regard. Discuss and analyze the material collected with representatives of the center of consciousness. The most powerful antidote to being possessed by the unacknowledged shadow material is to air it out. If the center of consciousness can acknowledge the repression of values and attributes of one or more *minority* groups, it can then move *choicefully*, with forgiveness and energy, to establish policies and procedures that can own the shadow material and lead to fundamental change.

Repression of the various "isms"—race, gender, age, able-*ness*—can be particularly tricky for an organization's center of consciousness to deal with. Clearly, no organization these days wants to embrace such attitudes consciously. But sadly they remain stubbornly rooted in the dark side of our society. For most organizations, the "isms" are relegated to the organization shadow. The problem is that, if the center of consciousness does not *know* that the relegation has occurred and that the "isms" are in fact a part of the psyche of all organizations in our society, it will be prone to acting out the "isms" in unconscious ways. The antidote is for the center of consciousness to acknowledge the realty of the relegation and to lead and manage the organization as though it were recovering from racism, sexism, age-*ism*.

Of course, the people who are marginalized in any particular organization may or may not be those disaffiliated in the society at large. In the larger society, the marginalized would include people of color, the poor, women, and other historically disadvantaged groups. However, in any particular organization, the voices that are not heard may have a different origin. For example, in some women's organizations, the male voice goes underground. In some religiously affiliated groups, people of the non-majority faith may stay quiet. So, it can useful to help the center of consciousness look around and notice if there are groups of whatever makeup in the organization that seem demoralized, alienated, cynical, or lacking in motivation and find out what is on the minds of their members. Another source of information about repressed energies can be those organization members who spend a lot of time in other organizations and who, therefore, may see things in the "back home" organization that the center of consciousness is not seeing.

Whole-organization change technologies, such as Open Space Technology and Future Search—which systematically seek out the wisdom of the entire organization—can also be important mechanisms for surfacing shadow material.

In Zone 3, Dealing with Organizational Complexes, whole-making work focuses chiefly on de-energizing organizational complexes that have pushed the organization in unhealthy directions or prevented it from undertaking necessary development.

Recall that a problematic organizational complex is often signaled by heightened and often long-standing feelings in the organization about some problem or issue. Such a complex can be addressed by gathering together a group of organization members representing the center of consciousness to identify the issues in the organization that are *too hot* to deal with. Facilitate a conversation about the feelings associated with these issues: When do the feelings arise? What behaviors are evident when the feelings are abroad? How long have such feelings been around? What archetypes might have been constellated by the feelings? Using the *Organizational and Team Culture Indicator*™ (OTCI™) instrument can help organization members understand the archetype at the root of the complex in terms of both its inherent values and strengths and of the organizational challenges it poses. This mapping of a piece of the organization's unconscious terrain can be therapeutic in and of itself. With the feelings sorted out and the behaviors understood and catalogued, the center of consciousness can also make choices about what new policies or procedures are necessary to move the organization out of the grips of *as if*.

Identifying the archetypal energy or myth at the center of a complex helps move the complex out of the unconscious into consciousness. When this occurs, the positive aspects of the complex can be strengthened and its counterproductive aspects weakened. Moreover, when the archetypal energy at the center of the complex is acknowledged at the conscious level, it has less need to hold the organization in its grip. This can allow more archetypal energies to express themselves, permitting more perspectives on reality and more information to be acknowledged. The result is decision making that is based on a more thorough analysis of the situation.

If the initial assessment indicates that the organization needs to change—but that the center of consciousness is *stuck*—it can be fruitful to work with representatives of the center of consciousness to identify the organization's founding myth or the myths surrounding its rebirth. These myths often carry archetypal energy that continues to feed and shape the organization—often in the form of a complex. Re-examining and re-experiencing the myths can give the center of consciousness perspective on the myths and provide the opportunity to grow and change.[8]

Sometimes a new leader can de-energize a problematic complex just by bringing fresh eyes to a situation, pointing out the compulsive or irrational behavior in an organization, and giving the center of consciousness permission to behave differently. This seems to have been the case at the Defense Personnel Support Center, an organization caught up in a negative Ruler complex that—in the mid-1980s—was keeping alive standards and procedures that dated back to the Civil War. A new administrator gave the organization permission to stop producing and stock-piling hundreds of millions of dollars of stuff that no one really wanted. A renaissance of cost-cutting and customer-pleasing action resulted.[9]

In Zone 4, on the Cusp of the Collective Unconscious whole-making is carried out largely through "processes of creative formulation."[10] Here the center of consciousness is given the opportunity to explore the power of the archetypal realm. In processes of creative formulation, representatives of an organization's center of consciousness are helped to identify the archetypes at work in the organization's unconscious; to assess the impact this archetypal energy is having on the day-to-day functioning of the organization; and to determine if any changes in culture, structure, or processes are indicated. While the representatives of the center of consciousness are experiencing the material that comes from the unconscious, they are invited not to explain or intellectualize the experience but to have the experience. Afterward, trying to make conscious sense of the experience, to move the insight from Kairos to Chronos, is critical to the process of moving toward wholeness. Processes of creative formulation focus on understanding opposites and how to move toward balancing and centering the organization within the tension of the opposites—in a sense how to invoke the transcendent function. They are processes that require the center of consciousness to let go of its need to be in control of everything and move some distance out of its comfort zone.

Approaches to creative formulation can be thought of as ways and means of welcoming and hosting the invited guest, the collective unconscious. They can include organizational active imagination—any technique by which the center of consciousness intentionally enters into dialogue with the Archetype of Organization, creative fantasy, work with organizational dreams or the dreams of organization members, the creation of symbols, art of all forms, drama, aesthetics, and even dance. Whole-making processes of this sort can help the center of consciousness move the organization closer to a full expression of its potential by engaging the four energies of the Archetype of Organization and by understanding the other archetypes that are active in the organization's psyche.

ENGAGING THE ARCHETYPE OF ORGANIZATION

If the initial assessment suggests that the center of consciousness is ready to begin engaging the organization unconscious but needs a basic orientation to organizational psychodynamics, try engaging a group representing the center of consciousness in a guided imagery exercise. Ask participants to visualize the organization as a psychological system: How does the organization present itself to the world? Where is the locus of controlling/directing energy? Is there a soul? What is the feel of the energy overall? Is there both light and dark energy? Ask individuals to capture their thoughts and images on paper. Follow up on this with a didactic presentation on the structure and dynamics of the organizational psyche.

If an initial assessment indicates the absence of one or more of the four major life energies in the psychodynamics of the organization, we have found it beneficial to use the *OTCI* instrument to set the stage for dialogue between the center of consciousness and the collective unconscious. The *OTCI* can help put names to the archetypal energies that are prominent in the organization's life, as well as those which are absent.[11] This naming, and an appreciation of the stories and myths behind the names, can lead to an analysis of the implications of the data for the healthy functioning of the organization. If the absence of an archetypal energy seems to be related to organizational dysfunction, the center of consciousness can "invite" new archetypal energy into the organization by engaging in new behaviors. For example, a *People* organization might discover that its quality control efforts are in disarray and that it lacks any *Results* energy. Instituting quality assurance procedures would be essential. Simultaneously cultivating the imagery of the Ruler showing concern for the welfare of his or her subjects would open the door to a flow of Ruler energy.

If an organization lacks a vision for itself, encourage representatives of the center of consciousness to put critical, analytical thinking on hold and engage the intuitive energies typically undervalued in organizational life. To do this, invite the representatives to use one of several art media—drawing, collage, etc.—to create symbolic representations of the future organization. Explicitly position this work as a process of tapping unutilized energy of the Archetype of Organization.

MORE OPEN-ENDED PROCESSES

▸ If the organization is in transition, it may report more experiences of the collective unconscious and the archetypes—signs and symbols, as it were. These could potentially yield clues for helping the organization make its transition. The consultant can pose this hypothesis, gather information in the organization about experiences of this sort, and then help representatives of the center of consciousness analyze those data for useful insights.

▸ Help the center of consciousness identify and understand contents of the organization unconscious using analogically mediated inquiry.[12] In this technique, organization members representative of the center of consciousness are asked to create analogs—drawings, sculptures, collages—of internal images of some aspect of organizational life. The consultant then helps interpret unconscious material that has been projected onto the analogs.

▸ If an organization is experiencing endings and beginnings, try creating rituals rich in symbolism appropriate to the organization that give voice to both the fears of letting go and the anticipation of moving on. Position this work explicitly as a means of tapping archetypal energy that can be unusually available during times of transition.

▸ If the organization is in the midst of culture change, it may find that the existing archetypal story needs to be reworked and retold. Encourage leaders in the organization to see themselves as the bridges between the old story and the new, embodying and speaking the virtues of both the old and new archetypes.

▸ If the center of consciousness is wrestling with an unresolved polarity, say between the need for stability or change on a particular issue, introduce the concept of the mandala—the magic circle containing polar opposites. Invite representatives of the center of consciousness to create with paper and crayons a mandala or mandalas that capture the polarity. Let the center of consciousness live with the mandalas visibly displayed for a period of time. Then reassemble the group to see if the transcendent function has yielded a unifying symbol or insight about how to resolve the polarity.

▶ If the organization has a dream—something that never quite happens, something just beyond its ability to bring off, but something frequently talked about in *if only* terms, give substance to it through dramatization. Ask organization members or outsiders to listen to the dream and then act it out in front of a group representative of the center of consciousness and organization members generally. After the enactment, create appropriate opportunities for those assembled to share new insights into the dream that might help it become a reality.

▶ Use mythic stories of legendary leaders and utopian organizations, e.g., the Arthurian legends of Camelot, to help an organization's center of consciousness ease into an encounter with the archetypal world. Work with representatives of the center of consciousness to identify which stage of this familiar tale—the call, initiation, trial by fire, illumination, or mastery—describes the organization's current story.[13]

▶ Utilize an understanding of synchronicity to recognize that when there is an external opportunity or constraint, there is a matching desire to respond to it in the unconscious life of the organization, if not in the consciousness of many people in the organization. When facing a new situation, assume it is axiomatic that there is already some part of the organization mobilizing to respond. Use guided fantasy or brainstorming with representatives of the center of consciousness to find where match between inner energy and outer challenge lies.

▶ If the organization faces culture change, remember that the qualities currently missing from the conscious life of the organization are available in its unconscious. The issue is not so much to get rid of an old pattern to make room for a new one, but rather to bring about a subtle shift in archetypal energies so that what was dominant in consciousness takes a secondary role, and potentialities that may lie dormant (or are being protected on the periphery of the organization by people who may seem marginalized) are allowed into the center of consciousness. Honoring the qualities that have historically dominated the consciousness of the organization, while at the same time acknowledging that these qualities may also have blindsided the organization, is more effective in bringing about change than demonizing the old qualities. If the old values are put down in the interest of selling others, resistance is certain to be constellated in those who identify with the old ways that are now being discounted.

▸ Use Open Space Technology (described in chapter 4) to address an organizational issue. In processing the outputs of the session, identify the ones that seem to carry archetypal energy. Name the archetypes. Discuss how the up-welling of this energy may be a response to one or more imbalances in the conscious processes of the organization.

THE PAYOFFS AND COSTS
OF MOVING TOWARD WHOLENESS

Consistent with the basic Jungian dynamic of polarity, entering intentionally into the world of whole-making brings both *good* and *bad* news to the center of consciousness. The *good news* is that by re-evaluating its public face, starting to own its shadow, withdrawing some of its projections, de-energizing some of its complexes, and listening to the wisdom of the collective unconscious, the center of consciousness can become increasingly comfortable with paradox, open to synchronicity, and alive to the dynamic balancing and rebalancing of energies that flow from and through the Archetype of Organization. All this psychodynamic work begins to free up energy and generativity in the organization that can rapidly show up in new and revitalized approaches to the work, the establishment of healthier relations with customers, and the creation of an internal work environment that is much more humane, vibrant, and morally responsive and responsible and that welcomes individuating organization members.

The *bad news* is that the process of organizational whole-making is never-ending. Whole-making is not a destination so much as a journey that yields only occasional glimpses of *organizational wholeness*. The organization incurs several costs by tapping into the energy of the unconscious. The first is having to endure a sense of continuous transition and "in-betweenness." The second cost is that growing awareness makes the center of consciousness ever more capable of seeing complexes that need to be de-energized and repressed material that needs to be dealt with. The third cost is that the Archetype of Organization and the collective unconscious do not always tell the center of consciousness what it wants to hear. The messages from the unconscious about what the organization needs to do to stay on the path toward *organizational wholeness* can be uncomfortable, stretching the organization's concept of what is possible and desirable, and pushing it to remain just a bit *out of control.*

If we think of the legend of King Midas, for example, we are reminded that both greed and a need for everything to be under control take the life out of life. The organization that allows for a freer flow of information and energy tends to foster an atmosphere that is alive, exciting, and responsive to changing needs and situations. Such organizations have access to so much more information than most that they are much better positioned to weather permanent white water—unless, that is, they get locked into too much "navel-gazing."

As with individuals in Jungian analysis, who should never substitute reflecting on their lives for living them, so with organizations. The reality, however, is that when an organization leaves behind the flavor-of-the-month approach to organization development in favor of an approach that includes mapping the organizational psyche and laying out strategies that allow for an ongoing process of research and action, both efficiency and aliveness are served.

Ultimately, the four zones of the organizational psyche need to be in relative alignment. If the public face is out of line with the organization's inner reality, the organization will be neurotic (just as an individual would be neurotic if he or she pretended to be one thing while really being another). If the organization's unconscious stuff is blocking the ability of the center of consciousness to see reality clearly and make healthy decisions, the situation is more like psychosis. If the center of consciousness ignores the existence of the collective unconscious, its connection to its creative source is disrupted. The result can be a sense of emptiness, meaninglessness, and stultification that results in a failure to innovate and keep up with changing times. The strategies outlined in this chapter can heighten consciousness in each zone of the organizational psyche, making it possible for an organization's leaders to foster an environment of psychological balance and wholeness where the public face, center of consciousness, organization unconscious, and collective unconscious can work together for the good of the whole enterprise.

MAPPING AN ORGANIZATION'S PSYCHE

Continue, now, the process of using Jungian Organization Theory to map the psyche of an organization you know well and whose well-being matters to you. Turn to part two, answer the questions under task three, and record your answers on the accompanying worksheet.

Notes

1. Lepper (in Stein and Hollwitz,1992, p. 89).

2. Jung, *C.W.* 8 (cited by Stevens, 1991, p. 272).

3. Mark and Pearson (2001, pp. 41ff., 136, 345).

4. Cusumano and Selby (1995, p. 6).

5. Colman (in Stein and Hollwitz, 1992, p. 96).

6. White (1996).

7. Slater (1993, pp. 209-210).

8. McWhinney and Batista (1988) and Colman (in Stein and Hollwitz, 1992, p. 96).

9. Tyler (1997).

10. Jung (*C.W.* 8, cited by Stevens, 1991, p. 272).

11. The *Organizational and Team Culture Indicator* instrument (Pearson, in press) is an organizational archetype assessment tool that helps organization members better understand their organization's or team's culture by identifying the different—and some-times contradictory—myths or plots (archetypes) that shape the way it operates. The *OTCI* tool embraces the twelve human *faces* of the Archetype of Organization. The instru-ment organizes these twelve archetypes into four groups: *(Results)*—Hero, Revolutionary, and Magician; *(Learning)*—Innocent, Explorer, and Sage; *(People)*—Everyperson, Lover, and Jester; and *(Stabilizing)*—Caregiver, Creator, and Ruler. Each face of the Archetype of Organization has its own way of interpreting events and acting in the world. All twelve archetypal *faces* are valuable, and each brings with it a special gift. None is better or worse. The archetypal energies at work in an organization may change over time. The *OTCI* also prioritizes subscores that identify an organization's or team's values, strengths, and weaknesses.

12. Barry (1994).

13. Pearson and Seivert (1995).

CHAPTER SIX

Getting
Down
to Cases

In this chapter we present six organizational cases designed to provide the leader or consultant with concrete examples of how to map an organization's psyche and work with members of the organization to achieve pieces of *organizational wholeness*. Each case consists of the story, a Jungian assessment of the problems and possibilities, and a description of the whole-making intervention(s). Each case is either a synthesis of data from our experience with two or more organizations or a semi-fictionalized reflection of our work with a single organization, altered somewhat to protect the privacy of the client. While the cases are not in the narrow sense real, we think they are in powerful ways true to life. It is obviously impossible to provide a case to illustrate every dimension of the theories we have presented in this book. We hope, however, that these stories illustrate the uses of the principles well enough to guide you in applying them to an organization of your choosing.

Douglass College

The Story. Douglass College was established in the early 1960s by a consortium of religious and civil rights groups concerned that conventional four-year colleges were largely ignoring the higher educational needs of working adults, particularly in the African-American community. Douglass rapidly developed a fully accredited undergraduate degree completion program that allowed adults to pursue their careers while also pursuing their educations. The program was based on a balance between individual tutorial work that a student could carry out at home under the long-distance supervision of a Douglass faculty member and occasional seminars in which the learning community gathered for more traditional academic interaction. Douglass was an overnight success in the African-American community. The student body grew rapidly. Graduation rates started out and stayed high. Alumni and foundation money flowed freely into the Douglass coffers. One prestigious scholar after another knocked at the faculty door.

Despite these successes, the early years were marred by deeply emotional infighting between the faculty and the administration about core values and appropriate structures. Many of the faculty had been drawn to Douglass because it wasn't like the universities they had been at previously. They saw hope in the Douglass experiment for building an institution where learning was paramount and where creating a physical plant, dealing with educational politics, fund-raising, and institution-building took second place. The administrators were attracted to the possibilities inherent in creating a new kind of educational organization—and one that would endure. Their focus was on establishing institutional credibility, creating a physical place that people in the college and in the community could identify with, establishing a presence in the business community, and making a name for Douglass in higher education councils. In the end, the faculty prevailed, and Douglass went on to thrive despite its shaky business foundations.

Number-watchers in the administration started worrying about plateauing enrollment in the early 1980s, but the faculty downplayed the data, as the development staff was attracting enough money to balance the books and then some. A few administrators suggested re-looking at the distance learning strategy in light of new developments in computing and telecommunications, but they were discouraged from pursuing this by faculty members who said the original Douglass learning model was leading to exceptional educations for its participants.

Trouble started to develop in earnest in the late 1980s. Enrollment and revenues began falling. Administrators were concerned but, responding to faculty arguments that the college's reputation would carry the day, took no action. By the early 1990s, the downward trends had become dramatic, and drastic cost-cutting measures and faculty-downsizing became necessary. Morale among students and faculty sagged. Somewhat surprisingly to the administration, two prestigious traditional universities started dropping hints about buying Douglass and running it as an independent school. In 1995 the board of directors ordered an across-the-board assessment of internal operations and of the school's external environment.

The findings stunned everyone in the Douglass community. It turned out that while Douglass had stood pat with its long-standing approaches, two major waves had begun washing over higher education. First, corporate America had discovered in-house higher education as a tool for developing needed skills and also for attracting and retaining minority employees. More and more African-American adults who traditionally might have turned to Douglass for their educational needs were finding that they could get them met much more conveniently on the job. Second, the Internet had enticed a large number of organizations—including many traditional universities—into the distance learning arena, offering a wide array of higher education options. With a learning process based on the telephone/fax/e-mail technology, Douglass had fallen far behind in web-based applications. The board of directors hired a consultant to help the organization get back on the right track.

The Assessment. The archetypal Sage energy carried by the faculty had dominated the Douglass culture from the school's earliest days. In many ways, this made a great deal of sense for an institution of higher education, supporting as it did the search for freedom through understanding and creating a capacity for objective analysis of reality. The problem was that there was an absence of psychological checks and balances, and the Sage energy got out of control; its negative side—a disinterest in the mundane—came strongly into play, in a sense possessing the organizational psyche.

Reinforcing the emergence of the negative aspect of the Sage energy was the existence at Douglass of a negatively charged Ruler complex (Zone 3). While the positive energy of the Ruler powers the building of essential infrastructure, its negative side is often expressed in the resistance to change. Overloaded with negative associations, this complex made it impossible for the faculty—which dominated the organization's center of consciousness—to take a rational view of the non-academic side of organizational life. The results were two. First, Douglass suffered from an underdeveloped center of consciousness (Zone 2) that could not attend adequately to the necessary business functions of planning and forecasting and prevented the Sage energy from informing the organization's innate capacity to change and grow. Second, Douglass developed a public face which on the one hand transmitted an attractive image of intellectual excitement and meaningful adult learning—the conscious image, but also communicated the resistance to change that had become part of the organization's shadow—the unconscious message (Zone 1).

Whole-Making Process. The first order of business for the consultant was to help the center of consciousness come to understand that its own shortcomings and the mixed messages being sent by the organization's public face lay at the core of the university's problems. The key turned out to be using the *Organizational and Team Culture Indicator*™ (*OTCI*™) instrument with a group of senior faculty and administration members, which gave the Sage-dominated center of consciousness an analytical framework and a set of data it could utilize in detached self-inquiry. The data showed clearly that the organization's culture was too heavily influenced by the face of the Sage and that a focus on the counter-balancing energy of Ruler was the likely pathway to health. The consultant chose not to raise the issue of the complex directly because the discussion of the *OTCI* data drained much of the negative energy out of the complex. The insights gained from the *OTCI* discussion led to an examination of practical steps to shore up the organization's management processes, to move rapidly to integrate web-based teaching methodologies into the Douglass approach, and to re-engage with the university's core clientele through a sophisticated marketing campaign. Psychodynamically, this had the effect of purging the shadow messages being transmitted by the organization's public face

CENTRAL AVENUE COMMUNITY CHURCH

The Story. The Board of Elders of Central Avenue Community Church was sunk in despair. After nearly a hundred years, the church—a theologically middle-of-the-road protestant congregation—was facing the imminent possibility that it would have to close its doors permanently. The facts were clear: membership was down to 25 percent of what it had been in the church's glory days. Sunday morning worship rarely attracted more than 50 people, who got lost in a sanctuary built to hold 400. Annual contributions covered less than half the church's operating expenses, and the once robust endowment—tapped repeatedly to meet current needs—was nearly gone.

The board and numerous predecessor boards had wrestled endlessly with two fundamental realities: first, the once all-white, middle class community that surrounded Central Avenue Church had long since become a working-class black neighborhood; second, the church's black neighbors were at best only marginally interested in what Central Avenue Church did. Previous boards had gone on record year after year with commitments to creating a diverse worshiping community. They had endlessly, and with some frustration, speculated about what it would take to get *them* to come? What did *they* want? Why didn't *they* respond to our efforts to reach out with day-care programs, food and clothing closets, a second

Sunday morning service with an African-American character, and the hiring of a black associate minister? There was even an undercurrent of opinion in the church that *they* aren't showing gratitude for the sacrifices we're making on *their* behalf. Successive boards looked with exasperation and envy at a sister church down the street that—under similar circumstances—had transformed itself into a vibrant multiracial community.

The board was not able to see the symptomatic pattern in some other Central Church realities: the church had refused to interview black candidates for the senior minister job both times the job had become vacant in the previous fifteen years; only one person of color had ever chaired a church committee; the director of music refused to sing non-European music in the *main* Sunday service; the black associate minister's duties were limited to the *early* service and to the community outreach programs; no white members of the church were publicly involved in dealing with issues of racial injustice; the vast majority of the congregation's members drove to Central from faraway white suburbs. The black associate minister had contacts in the surrounding community who told him that the church's neighbors saw it as hugely hypocritical, but the board ignored his reports, blinded by its sense of all the good it saw the church doing and all the efforts the congregation was making to reach out. It was the associate minister who eventually suggested that Central needed outside help, and out of a sense of frustration and hopelessness, the board agreed.

The Assessment. Caregiver was the dominant archetypal motif at Central Avenue Church. In its ideal form this archetypal energy is in many ways a natural cultural underpinning for a Christian church.

Caregiver energy is about nurturing others and tending to the needs of the world. This face of the Archetype of Organization also has a sacrificial quality. This archetypal energy lay beneath the church's strong urge to reach out to help the surrounding community.

Yet within the archetypal energy of the Caregiver is a central tension. Caregiver energy is balanced by Care-receiver energy.[1] The Care-receiver can be constellated in any person or institution that needs assistance on account of age, health, poverty, disadvantage of any kind, or naiveté. When Caregiver energy is expressed in a healthy way in an organization, the tension between Caregiver and Care-receiver is recognized and held in an ongoing dynamic of giving and receiving. The tendency in many organizations energized by the Caregiver, however, is to overidentify with the abundance and power of the giver (Earth Mother or Earth Father) and to project the broken-ness of the Care-receiver onto the *other*.

In truth Central Avenue Church was in desperate need of help. The beauty of its archetypal urge to help was being corrupted by its projection of neediness onto the mostly black community, a pattern that is characteristic of the more liberal form of racism (Zone 1). (The uglier forms that racism takes project the *inferior, evil villain* onto the other.) The tip-offs to this dynamic included all the *they* language that peppered conversation in the church's governing councils; the near absence of African-Americans from church leadership; the carefully constrained role of the black associate minister; the hint of "second class-*ness*" surrounding the early service; and the cyclical, "we can't get anywhere with this problem" nature of the many efforts undertaken by the church to build a more diverse congregation.

The unacknowledged racist shadow was skewing the Caregiver energy by tainting the church's outreach efforts with a patronizing and subtly manipulative quality that spoke *we know best*. Sadly, in envying its sister church's success at creating a healthy multiracial community, the board of Central Avenue Church—essentially the center of consciousness—was projecting onto the other church its own innate but unrealized capacity for the same success.

Whole-Making Process. In agreeing to seek outside help, the board took the first step toward acknowledging Central's own neediness and beginning to withdraw the church's projections. The consultant the board hired suggested that several board members attend a workshop on eradicating racism offered at the local community college. The board members came back with some understanding of the church's unacknowledged racism and all the ways that this was unconsciously seeping into the church's programs. With these insights in hand, the consultant was able to open up a discussion with the whole board about the dynamic of repression, denial, and projection. The insights flowing from this work enabled the board to engage members of the surrounding community in a dialogue that started moving Central Avenue Church away from its unconscious patronization of its black neighbors to the beginnings of a community action partnership. Balanced Caregiver energy began to flow in the creation of new caring programs. Many problems remained to be solved, but the doors of Central Avenue Church did not close.

THE ALBERTA COMMUNITY COLLEGE DISTRICT

The Story. The Alberta Community College District came into being when an altruistic, humanitarian entrepreneur determined that his county needed a first-rate community college. He sought out community funding, traveled all over the country to recruit the best and the brightest professors, even seducing faculty from four-year colleges by offering a grand vision and high pay. He put together a powerful and committed board, including one key woman who personally made sure that the funding for the physical plant was adequate for truly beautiful buildings. The commitment was to offer the students in this community the very best in every way. Years later this small community college had grown to encompass numerous campuses with more than 100,000 students.

The success was truly phenomenal. Yet, after a number of years the original excitement and momentum had abated, and even many of the founding faculty had traded in their idealism for rather curmudgeonly cynicism. The public identity was fuzzy, as if in trying to be relevant, the college had tried to become all things to all people. Over the years, the campuses had become bureaucratic in the extreme, so that change occurred from the top down at a glacial pace. It was almost impossible to get things done.

Despite the general loss of passion, the college system still made a major difference in students' lives. Students talked openly about how when they were in need, the college was there, and how the work they did allowed them to find good jobs and put together excellent futures. Faculty stayed on, largely because the pay continued to be excellent, but also because of the ability to have a positive impact on so many young people. The college no longer felt so distinctive, but the mission was still satisfying to faculty and staff who cared about students. Moreover, there was still something cutting-edge about the college. It had brought in a noted expert in spirituality and education to do work with the faculty on clarifying their own values and teaching from them. A faculty group was working on culture issues, and overall, the campuses met the needs of their communities.

A member of the marketing staff became interested in archetypal branding and convinced the president to administer the *OTCI* instrument to all faculty and staff. The results indicated that the environment was still healthy and identified the top archetypes associated with the culture. There was basically nothing in the results that would be a public relations problem. However, the process itself revealed some issues within the college. It was six months after the original study before the top administrators allowed the distribution of an executive summary of the results or any discussion about it, even though most administrators who had access to the full, confidential report verified the apparent accuracy of the findings, based on their knowledge of the culture. Moreover, none identified any potential public relations problems surrounding publication of the data. Although the instrument was presented as one measure only, and although it had been made clear that everyone's views were welcome, whether or not they supported its findings, a number of people simply tried to invalidate the study by taking pot shots at the marketing professionals who commissioned the study. One highly placed administrator demanded the right to review all the original scan sheets personally. The level of paranoia seemed excessive for a place as fundamentally strong as this one.

The Assessment. The head of marketing called in a consultant to help college leaders think through the *OTCI* results and clarify the college's public face, or brand identity. The *OTCI* results indicated that Innocent, Ruler, Everyperson, Sage, and Hero energies were significant contributors to the culture of the college. All of these made sense: the Innocent reflected the attitude of students coming with the expectation that they were going to a place where they would learn what they needed to get ahead; the Ruler because of the size of the organization; the Everyperson because of the egalitarian community college mission; the Sage because the organization was a higher education institution; and the Hero because of the idealism surrounding the college's founding and its determination to be *the best*. However, the fact that none stood out reinforced the marketing team's concern that the public face of the college was not clear enough to be a rallying point internally or externally (Zone 1).

In considering the results, the faculty marketing team recognized that the archetypal energies of the Innocent and Ruler defined the organizational complex, determining that change would be slow, that there would be no surprises, and that innovation would be discouraged if it was not required for survival (Zone 3). Scores on three of the four quadrants of the Archetype of Organization (*Learning, People,* and *Stabilizing*) were high, but the *Results* quadrant lagged seriously behind. The marketing team recognized that this might be why it was so very hard to get things done.

A careful reading of the archetype descriptions led the team to the conclusion that the college evidenced the weaknesses of the Caregiver, the Innocent, the Everyperson and the Explorer. The team surmised that this translated into overly giving faculty and staff that might burn out; a tendency to denial; catch-22 bureaucratic situations, low expectations, and a tendency of individuals to exaggerate threats to their autonomy and pressures to conform.

As people with longevity with the college began to share its *sacred stories*—that is, the stories that seemed to epitomize its values and nature—they realized that they all had a Hero cast.

When asked to identify the optimal brand identity for the college, everyone involved concurred that the Hero captured who they were at their best. The most important role of the college was to empower students to take charge of their lives, and often in doing so, they were the rescue figures who helped people in their times of need. It became clear that the original

Hero identity had been lost as the organization got bigger and more developed. Reclaiming that identity gave it a whole new lease on life, so that it seemed more cohesive, youthful, and dynamic. Perhaps individuals taking pot shots at the study were evidencing Hero energy when disaffiliated from a clear vision, group goals, and a sense of idealism.

Their hope was that reinforcing the Hero energy through a strong brand identity might strengthen relative weakness in the *Results* quadrant. Moreover, the Hero's focus on the achievement of idealistic and ambitious goals might well galvanize the passions of the faculty and staff, helping them to forgo the joys of attacking one another while also re-inspiring those who were feeling dispirited and burned out.

Whole-Making Process. In promoting the Hero brand identity, this community college district not only changed its marketing messages, it also developed programs to reward faculty and staff for heroic efforts, to promote donors as hero-makers, and to streamline processes to promote a heroic results orientation. Over time, internal and external communications by major administrators reinforced heroism in all constituencies, while policies and procedures tangibly reinforced heroic efforts. Alumni who had the discipline and focus to make their own dreams come true were highlighted and were encouraged to mentor heroes in the making. The branding emphasis at the conscious level of the organization affected the unconscious, returning Hero energy to its primary role in the psyche of the organization. In this way, a branding exercise affected the felt identity of the whole organization.

A PLACE FOR SPECIAL KIDS

The Story. When Trevor McKnight created A Place for Special Kids (APSK), he had some original theories about child development and a passion for creating a haven for kids scarred by domestic violence. He had little if any knowledge about or interest in business. Trevor had himself been scarred by domestic violence in his childhood. This experience of a bad father gave him a profound empathy for the kids who came to APSK. That and a brilliant therapeutic approach produced a success rate which was the envy of other groups in the same line of work.

In many ways, APSK was an expression of Trevor's personal story, as well as of his marital and family dynamics. He was the organization's *big daddy.* Everything started and ended with him. He made all the decisions, from how to handle every case to what kind of paper towels to buy. His wife, Meg, was his loyal and trusted lieutenant, handling the business side of things under Trevor's close watch. Trevor's son Zack was a brilliant therapist who worked wonders with the kids. He and Trevor agreed about the kids and fought about everything else in what Zack termed "Dad's house."

Many employees came to APSK over the years. Attracted by Trevor's highly creative, even *avant garde* approach, therapists and social workers arrived with great excitement, learned a tremendous amount, worked hard on behalf of the kids, and then found, when they started to generate their own complementary notions, that their ideas were not wanted. They yearned and pushed for a more collegial environment with decision-making authority devolved to the professional staff, but they encountered unwillingness on Trevor's part to let go of control. Few lasted more than a year or so. Only Pete, a long-suffering friend of Trevor's from graduate school, managed to hang on. He had brought to the staff and to APSK's therapeutic program the *Myers-Briggs Type Indicator*® instrument and the concept of psychological types, the one *outside* idea that Trevor had allowed into the *family*. As retirement loomed for Trevor and his graduate school friend, it was not at all clear that the organization that had helped so many desperate kids would outlive its founder.

The Assessment. There were significant hints of Creator energy at work in the culture of APSK, but the dominant story was energized by the interplay of negative qualities of the Ruler aspect of the Archetype of Organization and the organization's overweening father complex (Zone 3).

Trevor loomed larger than life as the founder of APSK. By taking care of everything, from providing the theory and philosophy upon which the organization was grounded to deciding what kind of pens to buy, he helped to constellate the father archetype in the unconscious of APSK in its earliest days. His approach to managing the organization, although seen at some level by many employees benevolent despotism, was at bottom deeply resented by most. This provided a strongly negative charge to the organization's father complex that was only reinforced by the negative experiences Trevor and many of the APSK kids had had with their own fathers.

Trevor, the organization, and the organization's father complex were psychologically all inter-mixed. Trevor *was* APSK. And APSK suffered from being in identity with its father complex; it had become the complex. This potent psychological brew hamstrung the organization's operations. Certain choices were not possible or even discussable. It was a classic case of *my way or the highway*. The only way employees could deal with the situation was to acquiesce in a child-like manner, thus robbing the organization of its ability to grow—and grow up, or to leave. The sheer weight of Trevor's intellect and energy had kept the organization alive. But, if APSK were to have a future, the Trevor/father complex/negative Ruler knot would have to be untangled.

Whole-Making Process. Trevor's concerns about APSK's future led him to hire a consultant who specialized in the hand-off of family-owned businesses from one generation to the next. She saw a loose end in the organization's psychological knot and began to pull at it. The loose end was the concept of psychological types. Trevor and the APSK staff had over a period of many years developed a deep understanding of typology, including its relationship—via the inferior function—to the energies of the shadow and the archetypes. The consultant was able to help the staff translate these concepts into organizational terms, to embark on an exploration of the archetypal energies working in APSK, and ultimately to identify the organization's negative father complex. All this put some distance between Trevor, the negative father complex, and APSK the organization. Trevor was able to see the need to let go a bit. The organizational psyche could breathe again, drawing on more aspects of the Archetype of Organization than just the Ruler. The staff was then in a position to do some creative problem solving around how to position the organization for the future.

FAMILY SERVICES AGENCY MERGER

The Story. Two nonprofit family services agencies, A Second Chance and Safe Haven found themselves considering a merger. Three key considerations drove the discussions. First, the missions of the two organizations were almost identical, and it seemed as if combining forces would enable the joint team to do even more good than the two had previously done separately. Both organizations had solid finances, and the two mission statements were clear and compatible. Second, the CEO of A Second Chance was leaving, and her successor was not clear. It made a certain amount of sense to make a change at this time, since the head of Safe Haven was strong and committed to staying, even in the face of the efforts of a few disgruntled employees to undermine her. And, third, it appeared that the strengths of each organization might complement the weaknesses of the other.

A Second Chance had been founded as an offshoot of a government agency by leaders with backgrounds in the academic world. Perhaps as a result, this organization had highly developed administrative systems and hence was more bureaucratic than Safe Haven. It also placed more emphasis on research and on the development of new ideas and approaches. For example, it had often worked with parents—mothers and fathers—to help them become better parents, pioneering a new paradigm for working with troubled families. But, despite this pioneering instinct, the staff of this organization demonstrated little apparent interest in the merger.

Safe Haven had been developed by social workers, whose primary emphasis was legal advocacy and maintaining a superior shelter for battered women. It tended to see children and mothers in the more traditional way—as the victims of oppressive men—and emphasized shelter services and legal services to help women get custody of their children. It became very good at getting immediate results. At the same time, the staff was often hostile to management. In fact, the staff had gotten one CEO fired and was distracted by the efforts of a small group to discredit the current CEO.

The Assessment. The boards of the two organizations, encouraged by a savvy consultant, decided to administer the *OTCI* instrument to all personnel, hoping to identify whether there might be important culture issues that could undermine or strengthen the merger. The result showed that A Second Chance was a strong Sage organization, which also had a high level of Ruler energy that might, indeed, characterize its complex (Zone 3). This organization emphasized theory development and the implementation of new paradigms; and listened objectively to the data about the merger, waiting to discover how it would unfold.

Safe Haven had a strong Hero orientation, which allowed for courageous and forthright action. However, it also had a negative Everyperson complex that encouraged the group to band together against the leader (Zone 3). Moreover, the emphasis on *Results* was so much stronger than the potentially balancing concerns with *Learning, Stabilizing,* or *People* as to suggest a noticeable imbalance. Concern was expressed that A Second Chance might see itself as superior to Safe Haven, while Safe Haven might become oppositional to A Second Chance, seeing its cooler, more analytic atmosphere as elitist and deficient in care and concern. Similarly, it was feared that A Second Chance would simply ingest Safe Haven, obliterating anything that might be distinctive. However, it did look as if the organizations had complementary strengths. Safe Haven's strong *Results* orientation seemed to balance out the *Stabilizing* and *Learning* emphasis of A Second Chance.

The most surprising finding from using the *OTCI* tool was that both organizations shared the same shadow (Zone 2). For both organizations, Revolutionary energy figured prominently in describing the organizational weaknesses, that is, what the organization does that is counterproductive. Its more positive energies were also largely absent from the archetypal system of both organizations. The only archetypal face that was high for both organizations was the Magician, suggesting a fruitful common ground within a merged culture.

Whole-Making Process. The organizations decided to merge. They decided further to work intentionally to enhance the understanding of all stakeholders about the culture of their original organizations and to set about forming a new, joint culture very deliberately. The consultant first worked with each organization, using results from the *OTCI* instrument as a focus for discussion. Then the boards, management, and employees of both organizations went on retreat together to learn about each other's cultures and to consider how a true merger might work. The idea was to share a common language that allowed unconscious elements to enter common parlance. In this way, things that were normally shoved under the rug could be dealt with and discussed and anticipated projection defused.

In addition, the new organization chose to integrate the positive aspects of the Revolutionary into everyday experience. The leadership of the merged organization began this with a dress-down day, in which several key administrators came looking "cool" in a counter-cultural way. More profoundly, the leadership recognized that employees in both organizations were keenly aware of sexist attitudes in the larger culture and how these fed violence, incest, and other forms of family dysfunction. However, while A Second Chance had sometimes downplayed these insights to protect the objective image of the Sage researcher, Safe Haven, identifying as it did with the Hero, trumpeted them because it wanted to be seen as operating on behalf of society's values (as Heroes do). Both eventually realized that they had to honestly confront the larger questions, being willing to allow the public face of the new organization to reveal the Revolutionary beliefs that actually fueled their work.

The merged organization settled on the Magician as its archetypal face, unifying the can-do spirit of the Hero with the intelligent inquiry of the Sage. In doing this, the administration wisely came up with a brand identity that not only interested prospective donors but also helped to reinforce the parts of the organizational psyche that carried the most resonance and meaning for clients and employees (many of whom had once been clients).

The Magician leads through vision and needs no enemy, creating a sense of a future expansive enough to make a place for every valued current member. The new organization collected stories of ways each organization had empowered women, children, and rehabilitated or just stopped former male abusers. It then recast these stories portraying the merged organization in the guise of the Hero. Such stories inspired employees, reminding them why they go to work every morning. At the same time, the stories ennoble clients who might be currently down-and-out, but who want to make something of their lives. In making these choices, the leadership reconciled the new paradigm emphasis of A Second Chance with the result emphasis of Safe Haven.

DEFENSE INDUSTRIES GROUP

The Story. Defense Industry Group's problem was not profitability or, for that matter, success as measured by virtually any conventional yardstick. Far from it. DIG had made its mark during World War II as one of only a handful of companies supplying the U.S. military with avionics. Rapid acquisition of several rivals in the immediate postwar period positioned DIG for the dominant role it assumed in the industry in the early years of the Cold War, a position it had strengthened year after year. Profitability soared, payrolls expanded, and government-funded research produced a seemingly limitless array of new technology. DIG's position in the industry enabled it to continue to thrive even as military budgets shrunk in the 1990s.

One of DIG's historic strengths had been the large numbers of ex-military men the company employed. This gave the organization an insider's view of the market and instant access to and credibility with the "old boy network" in the Pentagon. Another strength was the company's single-minded focus on product quality and timeliness of delivery. Doing "whatever it takes" to get the product out the door became a company byword. A third strength was DIG's reputation for being unquestionably honest, but giving no quarter to the competition. This combination of traits had made DIG almost godlike in the minds of its customers and competitors. Its reputation for a determined bottom line focus made it a darling of the business school case writers.

DIG's problem was an organizational culture that had slowly begun to undermine the organization's ability to be an employer of choice, to attract and retain high quality designers and engineers—the lifeblood of long-term success. The downside of being staffed largely by former military personnel was a command and control culture that put the thinking largely in the hands of the management and asked that working-level employees do little more than be loyal and follow orders. This sat poorly with newer DIG employees, the *Gen X* crowd and the *Millennium Generation*, both groups famous for their inclination toward career "free agency" and their preference for democratic organizational structures. The heavy ascendency of men in the hierarchy put women and their career issues on the margins.

The few efforts pushed by DIG's human resources department to deal with these issues had proved ineffectual. Programs designed to engender more employee involvement and participative management had sparked snide managerial statements, such as: "Let's just get back to the real work and stop wasting time on all this process stuff." The nearly all-male hierarchy had proved loath to adopt flexible schedules, parental leave, and leave for eldercare. None of DIG's problems had showed up yet on the bottom line, but there was a growing sense at all levels of the organization that something wasn't quite right, that DIG's famous "can-do" attitude was somehow becoming a liability.

The Assessment. DIG was beginning to display the classic symptoms of an organization at the start of midlife. Up until this point, DIG had known only success piled on success. It had single-mindedly lived out the Hero archetypal story, in which focused energy, discipline, courage, and the ability to persevere when things got tough combined to help the hero overcome all obstacles and all enemies. Suddenly, and with no warning, what had worked so well for so long started began to fray at the edges.

Decades of single-mindedness had taken its toll. The energy of the organization was profoundly out of balance: *Results*-oriented energy had run roughshod over *People*-oriented energy, masculine energy had lorded it over the feminine; " command and salute" had undermined human freedom; control had squelched learning. DIG's very success had blinded the center of consciousness to the possibility that there might be another way. And the rebalancing process inherent in the organizational psyche had finally begun. The autonomous spirit of the Archetype of Organization had begun to speak through the people in the organization. The center of consciousness was beginning to get glimpses of all the possibilities of organization it discarded during DIG's push for success in the first part of its life (Zone 4).

DIG found itself at a choice point. Would it, like many organizations before it, choose to ignore the messages from its unconscious and try to go on as before. Or would it choose to engage the unconscious, its own shadow (Zone 3) and the collective unconscious (Zone 4), and begin the process of creating a healthier more balanced culture inspired and informed by the Archetype of Organization?

Whole-Making Process. An opening for change at DIG came when one of the company's senior vice presidents attended a leadership seminar in which the *System Stewardship Survey* was used to orient participants to their own leadership styles. The vice president came away with one important learning and one strong hunch. His learning was that his own leadership style was strongly influenced by *Results* energy and biased toward production systems to an extent that rendered him unbalanced as a leader. His hunch was that the management culture at DIG had a strong collective leaning toward Results that probably wasn't healthy and that might be at the root of the sense of uneasiness that he and other DIG leaders were beginning to feel about the company.

The vice president convinced DIG's chief operating officer to hire a consultant to work with the senior management team to assess the individual and collective leanings garnered by using the *System Stewardship Survey*. The results confirmed the vice president's hunch: the shapers of the DIG management culture almost to a *man* had marked leanings toward *Results* and had remarkably little inclination to pay attention to *People* issues. The group quickly grasped the system implications of their bias. While holding strongly to their focus on production as a key corporate value, they began to articulate and map out a set of interventions designed to focus management on fostering the growth of DIG's people and rethinking corporate values and processes with respect to the delegation of power and authority to working-level professionals.

MAPPING AN ORGANIZATION'S PSYCHE

Continue, now, the process of using Jungian Organization Theory to map the psyche of an organization you know well and whose well-being matters to you. Turn to part two and follow the directions under task four.

Notes

1. Pearson (1991) describes Care-receiver energy the "Orphan."

CHAPTER | **SEVEN**

Creating Wholeness:
Leading
the Organizational
Psyche

Creating the conditions in which an organization and its members can tap into the "soul stuff" out of which *organizational wholeness* can grow requires the combined efforts of all the leaders in an organization, managerial leaders as well as empowered individuals recognized within the organization as natural leaders. Managerial leaders, particularly the top person, may have easier and more natural access to the levers of power and the chambers of decision making, but all leaders share the burden and privilege of being stewards of the organization's psychological well-being.

Doing this work starts with a careful consideration of the assessment questions in part two. This will yield a clear picture of the organization's psyche and the kinds of whole-making processes best suited to its needs. Doing this work also imposes three additional disciplines on each leader: carrying out leadership as a spiritual pursuit; educating the organization's center of consciousness about the true nature of the organizational psyche; and serving as a catalyst for activating the spiritual potential of the organization. Taken together, these disciplines serve to open the organization to the workings of the transcendent function.

LEADERSHIP AS A SPIRITUAL UNDERTAKING

When people come together in organizations, we believe they give life to something that has an identity beyond the aggregate of the individuals involved. By constellating the Archetype of Organization, the creation of an organization opens the people in it to a shared experience of meaning that lies beyond their individual ego concerns. This communal connection through the organizational psyche/soul to the realm of the archetypes—the collective unconscious—gives organizational life a numinous quality.[1]

We believe it follows, then, that the leader who serves the interests of *organizational wholeness* is engaged in a deeply spiritual pursuit. This leader is called to serve a high cause indeed—ad*ministering* (*sic*) to the psyche, or soul, of an organization by creating the conditions in which the basic life forces can be channeled for productive purposes in the organization. This is not spiritual in any "out there," mystical sense, but rather in the sense of finding and honoring the deepest places of meaning in the organization and connecting them to the organizational here and now. Many leaders also report satisfaction in a mission of service, knowing that they are not just creating jobs for people, but making employment meaningful.

In our experience, the leaders who are the best stewards of this organizational soul seeking are those whose psyches and lives are in balance and who are personally committed to doing their own inner work. These leaders find that congruence and authenticity are of the essence in facilitating an organization's inward journey. They discover that the insight required to minister to the organizational psyche grows out of their openness to the mystery and transformative power of the unconscious in their own lives. They also discover as they do their own inner work—befriending their shadows and entering into dialogue with the archetypes—that their organizations mirror to some extent their own unconscious stuff. When the leader comes to terms with her once unconscious racism and reconsiders these attitudes, she changes. And suddenly she finds that without a big deal being made of it, she starts having more diversity in the workplace where she leads. When the leader discovers that certain archetypes strongly influence his behavior, while others seem absent from his life, he discovers how the processes of the organization where he leads are affected by those archetypal energies or their absence.

There are, of course, many possible approaches to this inner work. You may be far along your own path. If so, you already know the value of staying on it. If you have not begun, we offer several suggestions for getting started:

- Take the *Myers-Briggs Type Indicator*® (MBTI®) instrument to help determine the type preferences that determine how you prefer to live and work. You can then take the *Pearson-Marr*

Archetype Indicator™ (PMAI™) instrument to discover what archetypes motivate you and what narrative structures best explain how you typically make meaning of what is happening in your life. Of course, once you know this, you are in a position to notice the type preferences and the archetypal structures that you tend to de-emphasize or ignore. You can then learn from people who live out the positive expressions of your most-preferred type characteristics and archetypes.

▸ You may find it helpful to use the Archetype of Family Culture Chart in appendix D to explore the archetypal scripting you may have inherited from your family of origin. You might ask yourself this question: If your family were in a movie or a novel, what archetypal scene would it be? What archetypal part would you have been expected to play? When these patterns are made conscious, you can choose what positive legacies from your family to retain and pass on and what negative legacies should stop with you. Some leaders (and many organization members) find that they are unconsciously projecting onto the organization as if it were their family. Calling back those projections frees up enormous energy and allows for the recognition of new options.

▸ Pay attention to your dreams and fantasies, interpreting them as metaphoric or symbolic messages from the unconscious, helping to guide you in making creative workplace choices and to see patterns that you may ordinarily miss—in your own psyche and in the environment around you. When you are in a situation that is strikingly unusual and out of the ordinary, you may find it useful to interpret it symbolically, as you would a dream. For example, one woman, who had just bought a new car, ran it off the road in a storm. She replaced the totaled car with the insurance funds, and then a tree fell on the new car—again in a storm. While dealing with the practical details of again replacing the car, she also analyzed this experience as she would a dream. To her, the car was associated with the power to get places while storms were associated with tumultuous feelings. From this she decided that the reason she had been having trouble moving ahead with her life was that she had had to stuff her feelings over the past several years to get through some difficult times. Her analysis revealed that she had been having trouble moving ahead perhaps because she was stuck in the emotional turmoil of past difficulties. She concluded that she would have to deal with those feelings in order to get on with her life.

▶ When you feel disgust, great annoyance, anger, or judgment about someone—or an intense desire to please them—note that this emotional resonance is a sign that your shadow has been activated. If you take some time to think about this, you may be able to get a handle on the nature of your own shadow. You can start by simply writing lists of the qualities that make you dislike or adore someone. Then look at whether you have some of these qualities, or could be seen as having them by someone else looking at you from the outside.

▶ Take the *System Stewardship Survey* (appendix B) and the *Archetypal Leadership Styles Survey* (appendix C). Both instruments ask questions about leadership skills, preferences, and knowledge that can help users begin to understand which of the four organizational subsystems they are most comfortable with (and most skilled in dealing with). The *System Stewardship Survey* focuses on which of the four basic energies of the Archetype of Organization may be influencing a leader's actions. The *Archetypal Leadership Styles Survey* focuses on which human *faces* are mediating the four basic archetypal energies as the leader acts. It also identifies which of those energies are expressed in the leader's values and strengths.

▶ Finally, knowing that most of us are to some degree trapped by the stories we are living, you might make a practice of following what Native American leader Paula Underwood called "the rule of six."[2] Don't make any decision until you have told yourself six different stories about it. Several of these stories are likely to follow the plot lines of archetypes that are not normally dominant in your way of looking at the world. The desired result is freedom from being caught in the self-limiting thought loop that circumscribes the options of most people. As a leader, it is important to exercise the greatest possible flexibility in imagining options.

CREATING AWARENESS IN THE CENTER OF CONSCIOUSNESS

Central to the leader's efforts to create *organizational wholeness* is stimulating the organization's center of consciousness to become curious about itself and its relationship with the unconscious dimensions of the organization. Somehow, the center of consciousness must come to appreciate the value of the organization's inner complexity. Somehow, this organizational *ego* must be persuaded that the representation of the organizational psyche we offer in this book is a plausible and potentially useful tool for analyzing organizational psychodynamics. Somehow, the center of consciousness needs to see that the essential ingredients in the recipe for a healthy organization include understanding, honoring, and embracing the Archetype of Organization and the collective unconscious.

Just as the ego-centric ego of the individual must come to accept the limits of conscious striving before a person can embark on the journey of individuation, so the one-sidedness of the causal logic-focused center of consciousness must give way to an acceptance of the reality of the organization unconscious before the organization can re-member itself. This yielding hinges on the leader's ability to help the center of consciousness accept that there are limits on rationality, that there are aspects of organizational life that cannot be grasped by logic alone.[3] Acknowledging that there are behaviors within an organization that are out of ego control is key to making it possible for the center of consciousness to deal subsequently with the organization's unconscious processes.

For the leader in an organization where Jungian concepts are broadly understood—and there are a few—the analytical framework we have laid out in the preceding chapters becomes a natural tool for creating *organizational wholeness* on which the leader can readily draw. For the leader in an organization where the language of psychological types (for example, through use of the MBTI instrument) has taken hold, type concepts can provide a good base on which to build further awareness of the organizational psyche. A first step might be an exploration of the connection between individual typology and the shadow, helping organization members understand that an individual's inferior type function is relatively uncontrolled by the ego and often serves as a conduit for the movement of shadow material to consciousness. This could easily lead to a discussion about the nature of the shadow and its position in the unconscious of the individual. From there, it would not be too far a stretch to a discussion of the organization's shadow and other aspects of the organization unconscious.

For the leader in an organization that has neither an understanding nor appreciation of the unconscious realm, the task is, of course, much more difficult. The concepts laid out in this book are difficult for someone with a point of view steeped in scientific management. And the peculiar Jungian terminology can make the task even more difficult. We have found two other *languages* to be useful in helping the typical manager in the typical organization begin to *get* the Jungian concepts and in laying the groundwork for accessing the basic ideas we have presented. First is the language of energy. As noted previously, Jung insisted that the energy in human systems is the same as in all other systems—and that it is governed by the same laws of physics. Managers who have been trained in science and engineering can, in our experience, relate to the idea that psychic energy—which they may prefer to think of as "human will" or "intellectual band width"—is a function of polar opposites, much as electricity is. It can be blocked or dissipated by faulty engineering and *grid management,* and its natural reciprocating flow can be restored by appropriate managerial attention.

The second language that seems to help the translation of Jungian concepts into terms more accessible to managers is system thinking. Jung, of course, was a system theorist par excellence. He is seen as a member of the evolutionary or transformational school of system theorists, which also includes I. Prigogine, Ervin Laszlo, and Erich Jantsch.[4] Jung's model of the human psyche—upon which we have based our model of the organizational psyche—is a system replete with all the tensions and paradoxes around differentiation and integration, the parts and the whole, inputs and outputs, and the organizational system's relationship with its environment.

ACTIVATING THE SPIRITUAL POTENTIAL OF THE ORGANIZATION

The best way we have found to use system concepts in working with skeptical centers of consciousness is to conceptualize leadership as the process of stewarding and inspiriting four interlocking organizational subsystems that relate to the Archetype of Organization: the *production subsystem,* the *human community,* the *material subsystem,* and the *learning subsystem.*[5]

The *production subsystem* entails all the workings of the organization required to get the organization's products and services out the door. The production subsystem emphasizes the *where* and *when* of organizational life. It aims to ensure the organization's competitiveness and its ability to produce intended results. This is a focus on the *doing* energy of the organization and its quest for accomplishment. Ideally, this subsystem makes sure that the right things are done in the right sequence, on time, and in a manner that meets both the organization's and the customer's definition of success. It focuses on matching tasks to roles in order to maximize productivity and effectiveness, and on organizing people and tasks to create a winning team. The leader can inspirit the production subsystem by respecting the importance of mission and purpose among members of an organization and by paying careful attention to matching the talents and skills of organization members to the appropriate organizational role. When a person's role taps into her passion, energy is released, improving performance and preventing burnout. Showing such a concern communicates a sense that people have their own callings and that these callings matter. People who believe that their work is an expression of a higher purpose feel ennobled and spiritually fulfilled.

The *human community* is the interlocking web of interpersonal, intragroup, intergroup, and interdepartmental relationships that undergirds an organization. It focuses on the people in the organization and emphasizes the "who" of organizational life—who we are and how we relate to each other. This is a focus on the *relating* energy of the organization. Ideally, it helps people work together well, resulting in a sense of mutual care and respect. The leader can inspirit the human community by fostering genuine personal respect among organization members, providing opportunities for organization members to be known at deeper levels, helping organization members in conflict reach genuine understanding and reconciliation, and creating rituals that mark accomplishments and transitions.

As with the production subsystem, the human community may expand beyond the legal boundaries of the organization to include suppliers, customers, and everyone who has an ongoing relationship with people within the organization. The leader can infuse the human community with meaning by modeling an attitude of concern for people, by encouraging excellent customer service built on genuine care for the customer, by building deep and abiding relationships with markets, suppliers, and investors, and by treating employees with respect and even love.

The *material subsystem* encompasses such factors an organization's physical buildings and grounds—including their design and maintenance, financial record-keeping, all routine work, personnel policies and processes, and the aesthetics of the workplace. It emphasizes *what* is needed to accomplish the organization's mission. It focuses on the organization's stability, aiming to assure the continuity of the organization and the integration and predictability of its processes, internal systems, and structures. Ideally, the material subsystem is designed to foster an atmosphere of stability and ease, meeting the organization's need for vital equipment, comfortable surroundings, and appropriate pay and benefits. The leader can inspirit the material subsystem by helping organization members learn the Zen practice of mindfulness, being conscious and present while doing the mundane tasks of the workaday world. Organizations can measure and evaluate not only productivity, but also happiness . . . and perhaps the state of enlightenment of the organization.

The *learning subsystem* is the collection of processes, norms, and habits of mind that enable the organization to learn from its experience. It helps synthesize and apply knowledge that teaches organization members *how* to do their jobs. It focuses on the organization's boundaries and its relationship with its environment. Ideally it is the engine by which the organization continually adapts to a changing environment and by which it continually refines and improves its internal processes. The leader can inspirit the learning subsystem by encouraging an organizational vision that taps into both the Zeitgeist and the idealism of the organization's members, helping them feel that their activities make a difference in the world.

Each of the four subsystems is energized by one of the four great life forces embodied in the Archetype of Organization: the production subsystem by *Results* energy, the human community by *People* energy, the material subsystem by *Stabilizing* energy, and the learning subsystem by *Learning* energy. This means that, while the four organizational subsystems are—as noted above—interlocking, they are also in tension with each other. There are primary tensions between the production subsystem and the human community and between the material subsystem and the learning subsystem. The *Results* focus of the productivity subsystem sees human capital as something to spend, while the *People* orientation of the human community wants to nurture and develop it. The *Stabilizing* focus of the material subsystem wants to channel and control energy, while the *Learning* focus of the learning subsystem wants to let it flow freely in and around the organization.

THE MAGIC CIRCLE

None of the four subsystems alone makes for a whole organization. Each plays a role, perhaps even a dominant one at certain times and places—depending on the exigencies of organizational life; but, over the long run, significant imbalances among the subsystems have negative consequences for the organization as a whole. Leaders feed the different subsystems with their attentions. Too much or too little attention paid to any one of the subsystems will lead to organizational dysfunction. Too much attention paid to the production subsystem can create a *sweatshop* environment—too little can create a *country club*. Too much attention paid to the material subsystem can lead to stagnation, too little can lead to change for its own sake.

Most indigenous spiritual traditions emphasize the achievement of harmony with the natural, human, and spiritual worlds. One symbol of such balance is the magic circle or medicine wheel, traditionally composed of four revered directions and a sacred center. (See the discussion of the mandala later in this chapter.) We suggest using the image of the medicine wheel as a metaphor for understanding and achieving an optimal balance among and between an organization's subsystems. The four subsystems take the place of the four directions. Where the four subsystems flow together in the center is a place of creative, *both/and* tension. Seen through the lens of the objective and the day-to-day, this place of creative tension is where organizational politics determines which subsystems get what resources. Seen through a spiritual lens, this place of creative tension is where the organization's deep meaning lies within the wellspring of the organization's archetypal story, and the place in the organization's psyche where all the opposing forces create maximum pressure for integration into some fifth, unifying image or story (see figure 8).

THE LEADER AS STORYTELLER

We think that a key role of leadership is to be the keeper of the organizational story—about what the organization is, has been, and hopes to be—and that a critical part of inspiriting an organization is telling about the heroes of the past, characterizing the work organization members are doing now in ways that reinforce what the organization holds most precious, and bridging between the old story and the new. Leaders must provide a connection to the organization's legacy, highlighting what is best about the past, a role that satisfies the need of the soul for roots and meaning. At the same time, leaders must help articulate mutual aspirations, giving voice to

FIGURE 8 *Organizational Subsystems: Energized by the Archetype of Organization*

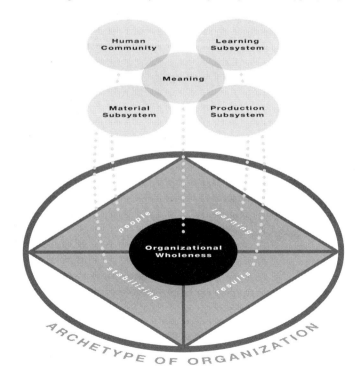

the spirit energy that can fuel forward momentum within a system.

This work implies that the benefits lie within not only telling the conscious story but also in listening for and telling the unconscious story. We suspect that when the inexplicable happens in organizations, an unconscious dynamic or story is often being played out. The leader who is able to discern the message from the unconscious in a disaster (Tailhook, for example) or in the serendipitous or synchronistic event (the emergence of a white knight who forestalls an unwelcome takeover attempt) can use this story to invite in neglected archetypal energies or type functions to the organization's conscious story. Honoring both the conscious and unconscious stories can be critical to creating an environment that allows people to bring their whole selves to work: mind, heart, will, body, and spirit—an environment that allows the basic life forces as embodied in the Archetype of Organization to move creatively in the conscious organization.

Organizational leaders are standard bearers; and the stories leaders tell, the impact of the deep plot structure of what leaders actually do, and the symbols leaders share can either unify organizational processes or fragment them. In a real sense, leaders are shamans and mythmakers for their organizations. Organization members tell stories about what leaders say and do that create the mythology that, for good or ill, informs the meaning structure of the organization.

The more consciously leaders hold this power, of course, the better. As every archetype has a negative as well as a positive side, consciously telling stories and using symbols that position an organization's key archetype at its positive pole strengthens its productive expression. When counterproductive archetypal behaviors are evidenced in the organization, leaders can remember to redirect the energy of that archetype to its more positive form through what they do and say.

In addition to telling stories that reinforce the dominant archetypes—in order to anchor the organization to its core meaning and reason for being—it is also important for leaders to encourage the small movements required to steer a craft in shifting seas, adjusting the organization's emphasis to the direction of the wind and the movement of the waves to keep the ship upright and afloat. Leaders can also avoid potential storms by keeping their peripheral vision tuned in to developments in the external market and the internal organizational dynamics. To compensate for blind spots, a leader may want to engage the help of consultants or other key players in the organization who have a different perspective and therefore may notice what the leader might ignore.

Most important, when trouble seems to be brewing, it is critical for leaders to take a moment or two to go inward and reflect. For example, this can include a quick review of the mapping you are doing of your organization and yourself in this book. (Some may find it helpful to keep those maps close at hand for just such times.) Taking a moment to diagnose the situation before acting can prevent missteps; it can also assure that action taken, however atypical it might be, is best matched to the challenge facing the organization.

OPENING THE ORGANIZATION
TO THE TRANSCENDENT FUNCTION

Broadly speaking, the leader pursuing *organizational wholeness* can be seen as the agent of the transcendent function. Jung, who coined the term in describing the dynamics of an individual's psyche, suggested that the transcendent function is a natural process by which the energy field created by the tension between the ego and the unconscious is brought into equilibrium.[6] The transcendent function does its work when the ego and the archetypal Self *agree to disagree* on some issue—perhaps a dream has suggested a course of action troubling to the ego. The transcendent function holds the tension between ego and Self, allowing the collective unconscious the opportunity to produce a symbol that points to a course of action, not previously considered, that unifies the opposites.

We think the transcendent function also works in the organizational psyche. In organizational terms, the transcendent function can be understood as an autonomous process by which the organizational psyche holds the tension between the desires of the center of consciousness and the desires of the organization unconscious—or between any two divergent points of view deeply rooted in an organization—until a symbol or concept emerges that bridges the tension and unblocks the organization's progress toward greater wholeness.

Organizational scientist Edwin Olson was the first to suggest that the transcendent function operates in organizational life. He describes how the transcendent function helped an experiential training group to break out of an impasse between fast-hardening factions that threatened to block the group's development. One faction wanted to use the group's time to compare experiences from their respective workplaces. Another faction wanted to use the group's time to disclose personal material and receive feedback from other group members. The group was stalled. Then an unaligned group member gave another group member feedback about something that had happened in real time in the group. The impasse began to dissolve as members of the two factions saw a third possibility for how to use the group's time emerge before their eyes, namely using their time in the group to deal with each other in the here and now.[7] Olson's role, as the leader of the group, was to hold the tension of the opposites in the group's psyche until the third way emerged.

As in Olson's group example, an organization is most likely to encounter the transcendent function when it is wrapped up in internal conflict between apparently irreconcilable points of view. Southwest Airlines again provides an example. Some years back, management found itself caught in a bind. On one side was tough competition from other airlines that was forcing Southwest to cut costs and keep them low. On the other side were the labor unions, pushing for better pay and long-term job security. For other airlines, this conflict had resulted in strikes, disruption of operations, and animosity between management and labor. Southwest went down a different path. The organization's leadership held the tension of the opposites until all parties came to see that their apparently divergent interests could be met by a *third* way: a joint commitment to increasing productivity through continuous improvement and change has brought the company growing competitiveness and its workforce steadily rising salaries and stable employment.[8]

The best outcomes in cases where fundamental differences, perhaps two equally plausible paths, are on the table in an organization often have a strong symbolic quality about them. The Baltimore Orioles' baseball stadium—which blends state-of-the-art technology with a *retro* design and a location in Baltimore's gritty industrial area—has created a powerful symbol positioned in the heart of the city. This symbol may not in a narrow sense be a product of the transcendent function at work in organizational life. But the immediate public identification with and affection for the stadium suggests the kind of powerful, union-of-opposites energy that is typically an outcome of this process.

The mandala, referred to earlier in the description of the Archetype of Organization, has a special place in the work of the transcendent function. The balancing symbols produced by the action of the transcendent function may often take this form. *Mandala* from the Sanskrit translates as *center, circumference,* and *magic circle.* It is often depicted as a square enclosed by a circle (as in a baseball stadium). Jung saw the autonomous appearance of mandalas in dreams, active imagination, and the arts as evidence that movement toward wholeness was taking place.[9]

Jung did not intend to suggest anything metaphysical in the use of the word transcendent. He merely meant that this function facilitates a transition from one attitude—the unconsciousness—to another—consciousness.[10] Leadership is the agent in the life of an organization that creates the necessary conditions for this transition to occur—essentially one of moving knowledge and energy from level to level. And, while transcendence in this context does not imply moving beyond material existence, it clearly implies that leaders need to rise above the limits of action conventionally assigned to the leadership role in organizations. It is leadership that recognizes the need for change, recognizes that the usual either/or debate is not going to resolve the issue, and helps create the tension in the dialogue between the center of consciousness and the Archetype of Organization from which transformational change can emerge.

We believe that leaders can invoke the transcendent function only by positioning themselves psychologically at the center of the organizational medicine wheel/mandala. The center is where the leader identifies the polarities in the organization and holds them in tension against each other so that new possibilities can be created. Between the opposites of organizational life is where the leader is inexplicably "with the stream" of the organization's energy[11]. Holding the tension of the opposites is perhaps the ultimate in trusting the process, in this case the process built into the organizational psyche that leads to *organizational wholeness.*

LEADERSHIP AND CONSCIOUSNESS

Most leaders have a desire to know and understand more, and they have had experiences that demonstrate to them how easy it is to miss information that is right under their noses—especially if it does not fit their expectations. It is difficult to anticipate what you do not expect, even when you have enough information to do so. The theories and ideas laid out in this book can help leaders and leadership teams become more conscious of their expectations and habitual ways of thinking and acting and more open to the autonomous unconscious thought processes in themselves and in their organizations. This in turn can bolster the ability to think the unthinkable (good or bad) and hence more adequately anticipate future trends. The need to do so is obvious enough in a highly competitive, fast-paced environment that shows no signs of slowing down or becoming any less challenging

MAPPING AN ORGANIZATION'S PSYCHE

Continue, now, the process of using Jungian Organization Theory to better understand an organization you know well and whose well-being matters to you. Shifting your focus a bit to your relationship to this organization as a leader, turn to part two, answer the questions under task five/steps one, two, and three. Record your answers on the accompanying worksheets.

Notes

1. Pearson (1998).

2. From a conversation between Carol Pearson and Judy Brown, consultant and educator in private practice in Hyattsville, Maryland (2001).

3. Corlett (2000).

4. McWhinney (1991).

5. Pearson (1998).

6. Wilmer (1987, p. 184).

7. Olson (in Stein and Hollwitz, 1992, pp. 158-162).

8. Tyler (1997).

9. Fincher (1991, pp. 1, 2).

10. Wilmer (1987, p. 184).

11. Jantsch (1975, p. xiv).

CHAPTER EIGHT

Restoring Wholeness:
Consulting
to the **Organizational Psyche**

An organization intent on beginning and staying on the journey toward *organizational wholeness* may very well, like many individuals on the path of individuation, find that it needs some help. An organization's psychopomp, or *psyche escort,* will often be an external consultant. The task-oriented, objective work of this consultant is the mapping of the organization's psyche, a process laid out in part two of this book. This chapter explores some of the process-oriented challenges facing the consultant, and some issues of ethics and integrity that we believe are key to a healthy consulting relationship.

THE ISSUE OF READINESS

Assuming that the organization has not stumbled unintentionally into the unconscious realm (a situation that would of course require immediate attention from the consultant to help make these energies as conscious as possible to protect the organization from harm), determining an organization's readiness to deal with its whole psyche, and in particular to engage the unconscious, is a critical part of the assessment process. There must be an accurate evaluation of whether the center of consciousness is at a point in its development where an encounter with the organization unconscious is appropriate or even possible.

If the center of consciousness is relatively undeveloped—immature, indecisive, unfocused, or divided—dealing with unconscious material could be overwhelming or even harmful to the organization, surfacing issues and images that could frighten and confuse the organization and its members. This is especially true if there is reason to believe that key players have significant, untreated emotional or mental problems or active addictions.

If the center of consciousness is well developed but in denial about the reality of the unconscious energies in the organization, then a full-blown Jungian approach may simply not be politically tenable. It may still be possible, however, to utilize assessment instruments such as the *Myers-Briggs Type Indicator®* or the *Organizational and Team Culture Indicator™* instruments. Appropriately framed, these tools can provide such an organization with some useful insights into its behavior, even though the organization may have an imperfect understanding of the tools' meanings and uses.

If the center of consciousness is willing to begin the journey, the approach outlined in *Mapping the Organizational Psyche* can be a powerful diagnostic that can be used in planning and change efforts, the creation of branding and marketing strategies, leadership development, team-building, and organization development projects. It can also aid in ongoing quality assurance evaluations. Organization members are most likely to be open to such a depth approach when they see how it can contribute to conducting these ordinary activities in a more thorough and effective way.

A PARTNERSHIP MODEL

In a Jungian approach to consulting, the client and consultant work as collaborators and partners. This is the antithesis of the *expert* approach to consulting, in which the *consultant* is expected to provide the answer. Out of the dialogue between client and consultant, a third point of view emerges, a redefinition of the problem/situation that opens the way to action. In Jungian organizational work the client and the consultant both bring important perspectives, knowledge, and competencies to bear. For this reason, it is ideal for the consultant and the client organization to work together through the assessment of the organization suggested in this book.

The client owns the problem/situation, sees it from the inside *out*, and serves as the expert on the organization. Ideally, the client organization invites the consultant into the partnership. The client must want to do the developmental work and must understand that the work will have a strongly heuristic character—helping the organization to come to understand itself. In Jung-oriented interventions, the client organization is not so much told about itself as given an opportunity to get in touch with itself. A good consultant in the Jungian mode is a person in the presence of whom good things happen.[1] But, at the end of the day, only the organization, particularly its center of consciousness, can make organizational whole-making a reality.

The consultant sees the problem/situation from the outside *in* and is the expert on a set of processes and techniques that can help guide and shape the course of the organization's development. The consultant is the partnering outsider, who thinks outside the box simply because he or she *is* outside the box. Especially when dealing with unconscious elements— e.g., the complex, the shadow, or projection, the client may have real difficulty in seeing what is going on, precisely because these dynamics are unconscious. To an outsider, however, they are often readily apparent. Of course, the consultant must take care not to shock the system of an organization by forcing people to see what they are highly resistant to seeing. Doing so may even lead to the consultant being fired or scapegoated. Timing is the key. Since insiders have a tendency to take for granted what is *right* about their organization, the consultant, happily, is also in a good position—as an outsider—to recognize what is working in an organization. Shoring up awareness about the strengths of an organization helps bolster the center of consciousness, making it more open to facing up to difficulties and blind spots.

FOUR KEY CONSULTANT ROLES

The consultant plays four key roles that help create the opportunities for whole-making to occur: *troubadour, catalyst, container,* and *wounded healer.* As *troubadour,* the consultant spreads the news about the state of other organizations, reminding people that most problems found in their workplaces are not so shameful. They are ordinary and human. There is no organization that lacks a shadow or a complex, and there is no organization that is immune from expressing the negative sides of archetypes or the undeveloped sides of nonpreferred type functions. All these problems are ordinary ones. The more an organization is willing to look at them and make them conscious, the healthier the organization becomes. The consultant as troubadour helps an organization move through its resistance by normalizing its shortcomings, moving it to a place where it can change.

As *catalyst,* the consultant stimulates the interaction between the levels of the organizational psyche, serving as a go-between, engendering opportunities for dialogue between the center of consciousness and the Archetype of Organization or other archetypes. It is helpful in this catalyst role when the consultant has access to the archetypal energy that is most crucial to the organization's historic sense of itself, as well as to the archetypal energy that needs to be brought into the organization's processes in the moment.

While the consultant should as much as possible stay out of the action and avoid pursuing a personal agenda, unavoidably, some of the consultant's own unconscious *stuff* will get intermingled with the organization's psychodynamics. The consultant and client organization will almost inevitably become engaged to some degree in transference and countertransference.

Transference occurs when the organization and/or individuals in it transfer to the consultant feelings generated by past experience with other people or by archetypal energies. The consultant could, for example, evoke feeling-toned memories among organization members about a *wise old man* figure who used to play a key role in the organization's leadership. These feelings could offer a useful cachet, but they could also hobble the consultant with unfair expectations.

Countertransference occurs when the consultant projects complexes onto the client or the client organization. Consultants are not infrequently called into situations that call up their own *stuff,* and the consulting process can be an opportunity to work with those issues. For example, the client reminds the consultant of his or her overbearing father. To work well with the client, the consultant will have to deal with this resentment being careful not to inadvertently reenact childhood or adolescent responses in the midst of trying to perform the consulting job.

If both consultant and client can maintain reasonable objectivity, and as long as the intermingling of unconscious energy helps move the organization toward greater awareness, the intermingling is probably all to the good. It is, in some measure, the new energy field that develops between the consultant and the client organization that helps create novel psychological insights for the organization. Consultants often embody the very qualities the organization needs.

For the consultant, while it is essential to put primary emphasis on the client's needs, every consultation provides an opportunity for personal growth. Doing organizational work out of a Jungian stance may in fact foster the consultant's individuation process. The client organization may well embody some of the qualities the consultant needs, and as the consultant learns to appreciate and connect with the client where the client is, he or she also heals personally. The relationship between the consultant and the flow of archetypal energy that can be loosed in the organization by whole-making processes is an intimate one—even alchemical—and the consultant can expect to be changed by the processes he or she sets in motion.

Both the client and the consultant need to monitor the dynamics of transference and countertransference closely. They become a problem only if the consultant's unconscious material blocks his or her understanding of the organization's situation or acts as a drag on the organization's development—for example, by rendering the organization dependent on the consultant.

As a *container,* the consultant creates a *temenos,* a psychologically safe place in which the change process can take place. In playing this role, the consultant helps the center of consciousness to draw and maintain a safe and secure boundary around the developmental process. This boundary creating works to moderate the flow of energy back and forth between organizational consciousness and the organization unconscious, to hold the tensions between the poles of the opposites until the organization unconscious begins producing symbols and images that can move the organization a bit closer to wholeness, and to protect the organization members who participate in the work from reprisal.

As *wounded healer* the consultant brings a necessary paradox into the consulting process. The wounded healer is an image of opposites, "woundedness" in tension with the capacity for healing. The consultant who hides his "woundedness" removes that potentially valuable part of himself from the interaction with the client organization. The consultant who honors the wounded healer archetype acknowledges both the whole and broken parts of herself and can therefore see both parts of the client organization.[2] Both the consultant and the client organization need to acknowledge their imperfections—neither has all the answers.

By asking for help, an organization in a real sense acknowledges its neediness—maybe even its brokenness. In the spirit of partnership, the consultant needs to reciprocate. This does not mean that the consultant needs to strip himself psychologically bare. Doing too much sharing about one's own issues may put the client organization in the uncomfortable position of feeling it needs to take care of the consultant. The middle ground is to share what is relevant and helpful in setting a tone of realness and partnership. Even if the consultant does not explicitly talk about her own travails, an attitude of nonjudgmental empathy and compassion says a great deal. It says the consultant has been there and that he knows what it is like to be struggling.

THE LITMUS TEST OF LOVE

Above all in the consulting process, the consultant must operate out of the love principle. For Jung, "love is the force that binds the opposites."[3] And the consultant striving to bring Jungian principles to bear in his work must

Temenos

Temenos, the Greek word for container, connotes the safe place that the consultant and the organizational client need to co-create for the work of organizational whole-making. *Temenos* literally means a piece of land set off as sacred ground—a temple enclosure, a grove dedicated to a god or goddess, or the center of a ceremonial circle. In ancient times, healing rituals took place in this protected setting.[4]

Translating *temenos* into the realm of psychology, Jung used the word to mean the *psychodynamic container* created during analysis by the analyst and client. Used this way, temenos embraces the honoring of the

▸ ▸ ▸

103

unconscious, the reciprocal trust, and the confidentiality necessary for supporting an individual's transformation.[5] Jung also writes about the archetypal self as having the quality of a "numinous temenos."[6] *Temenos* does not, however, connote only warm and cozy. It also means a place that is safe for asking and answering penetrating questions, speaking and owning home truths.

Given the rational, or conscious, bias in most organizations, dealing with unconscious material is potentially risky business for organization members at whatever level of an organization's hierarchy. Creating a politically and psychologically safe place for this work is obviously critical. Moreover, in light of the "soul-searching" nature of Jungian organization work, it seems highly appropriate for the consultant and client to prepare this organizational *temenos* with the spiritual nature of the whole-making process very much in mind.

understand the centrality of love. The consultant who cannot love the client organization and its people cannot help it or them. We call this the consultant's litmus test of love. This is not to say, of course, that the consultant should be in love with the client. That is an *as if* state in which the consultant lacks essential objectivity about the client organization's needs. Rather, we mean love as a deep-seated commitment to caring about and standing by the client organization as it moves toward organizational wholeness.

CONSULTING WITH INTEGRITY

As with leaders of organizations, consultants can gain the level of clarity required to consult well using Jungian models only by doing their own inner work and by recognizing their own parts in any difficult encounter in working with clients. The consultant who is afraid of or unaware of his or her own unconscious material can be of little use to a client organization with needs in the psychodynamic realm.

In order to do this work with integrity, it is important for the consultant to understand her own psychological type—including its biases; the nature and limits of her persona; the archetype(s) that currently determine her way of making meaning in the world; the complex(es) that may trip her up and limit her awareness; and her own predilection to emphasize results, people, stability, or learning. It is also important for the consultant to have some mechanism for connecting with her personal unconscious and with the collective unconscious. Analyzing one's dreams, doing active imagination exercises, being in analysis or other depth-oriented psychotherapy, journaling, or conscious artistic expression (painting, composing, movement, etc.) are just some of the ways the consultant can make unconscious dynamics conscious. These, as well as other personal disciplines, are necessary to guard against a tendency toward inflation that can bedevil the person working to heal the collective.[7]

Consulting with integrity also requires the consultant to understand that he cannot lead clients where he has never been or is afraid to go. If the work with a client requires it, the consultant will need to be able to go to the next level of resolving his issues with his mother, father, ex-spouse, or enemy; face a new realization about his own shadow; or step out of his own comfort zone to act or speak in nonhabitual ways. And if the consultant cannot do this work, it is important that he refer the client to someone who can or whose issues are not triggered by this client.

It is also important for the consultant to have a clearly defined ethic. Sometimes organizations get into trouble because they are willing to compromise too many of their values to the bottom line. Of course, when that happens, morale plummets. It is therefore critical that consultants have clear moral boundaries and are willing to quit a consulting job, even if it means losing income. Conversely, in the nonprofit world especially, sometimes organizations are so focused on their missions that they forget the issue of sustainability. It is therefore essential that consultants model requiring a reasonable fee for their services.

CONSULTING AS A TRADE,
A SCIENCE, AND A SPIRITUAL ENDEAVOR

Working with the organizational psyche—soul—has practical, scientific, and spiritual dimensions. It is a practical pursuit, in that, much like a plumber or electrician, the consultant seeks to unplug and unsnarl the organization's pipes and wiring so that blocked energy can flow again toward productive ends. It is important, then, for the consultant not to substitute the issues and dynamics clogging his own psyche for those the organization already suffers from.

It is a scientific undertaking, in that the practitioner must operate as a hard-nosed, rational, objective collector and analyst of data. Consultants with ego strength and the capacity to deal with their feelings without being overwhelmed are best able to serve their clients. Remaining objective allows the consultant to see the emotions that are triggered in himself by the consulting process as data that can help explain the forces being constellated in the client organization. Jung himself went through a period of psychological difficulty in which he was able to bracket and continue his work, grappling with the emotional issues that were raised during the day when he had space for himself in the evening.[8] The ideal consultant will recognize personal feelings as the work unfolds, but rather than being over-taken by them will use them as important data in the consulting process.

It is a spiritual pursuit because the consultant works in the imaginal space of the organization to connect the organization to its soul, its inner-most source of meaning and potential. With his spiritual hat on, the consultant must proceed with a certain necessary naïveté, vulnerability, and openness . . . in awe of the mystery of the human experience in organizations.

In the end, organizational whole-making cannot be accomplished through elegant words or clever technique. We think that—beyond a general orientation—one cannot learn much about organizational healing from this book, or any book. The key to successful whole-making lies in the personal integrity of the consultant. The best practitioners of the organizational arts suggested in this book will be those consultants who are deeply committed to their own journeys of individuation and who have reached that point in life where work and fun largely overlap. The richest source of ideas for how to engage with the organizational psyche will almost certainly turn out to be the experiences of consultants in their own personal journeys toward wholeness.

Each consultant will ultimately write her own "soul book" for facilitating organizational healing, describing processes of understanding and processes of creative formulation that emerge from her own inner journey. Whole-making from a Jungian stance is for all intents and purposes a new art form. Much exciting and uncharted territory lies ahead as "whole-makers" and the organizations they serve experience the paradoxical nature of the trip into the unconscious.[9]

MAPPING AN ORGANIZATION'S PSYCHE

Continue, now, the process of using Jungian Organization Theory to better understand an organization you know well and whose well-being matters to you. Shifting your focus a bit to your relationship to this organization as a consultant, turn to part two, answer the questions under task six/steps one and two, and record your answers on the accompanying worksheets.

Notes

1. Johnson (1999), describing the role of the Jungian analyst, inspired this idea.

2. Samuels (1985, p. 187) and Wilmer (1987, pp. 117–125) influenced our thinking about the connection between the wounded healer archetype and the work of the organizational consultant.

3. Jung (*C.W. 16,* para. 398).

4. Wilmer (1987, p. 89)

5. Samuels (1986, cited by Olson, in Stein and Hollwitz, 1992, p. 170).

6. Wilmer (1987, p. 89).

7. Robert Johnson voiced this concern about inflation in a private conversation with John Corlett in 1996.

8. Jung (1965).

9. Johnson (1989).

CHAPTER | NINE

Hermetic
Transformation

Many organizations still persist in thinking that both the source of and the solution to their problems lie primarily *out there*. These organizations continue unconsciously to project their own unresolved conflicts and un-addressed shortcomings onto their own employees or onto other entities, and mistakenly see these negatives as residing in the *other*. They continue to insist on searching *out there* for the answers to the question: "How do we become more relevant, more effective?" Leaders have grasped at one anodyne prescription for organizational health after another. In pursuing these nostrums, organizations have followed a tendency widespread in American society to engage life superficially and in a largely unconscious, reactive mode. And they have forfeited the possibility of organizational renewal that can come about when the center of consciousness starts to reflect on the organization's unconscious *stuff*.

The organizations most vulnerable to getting into this kind of trouble—and, regrettably they are legion—are those we would call patriarchal, after the macho (or false masculine) values, norms, and behavioral styles that predominate in them. The patriarchs running them, men and women alike, defend a one-sided, but deeply held set of *shoulds* and *oughts* about creating and maintaining their organizations. Their dictums are often grounded in a worldview that sees the universe as a wind-up clock; living organisms as machines; life as a competitive struggle; and unlimited economic and technical growth as a viable long-term strategy for humankind.[1] This is the quintessential Cartesian/Newtonian mind set— the linear, cause-and-effect, reductionist logic of the scientific revolution and of our modern techno-civilization. It is sustainable only by assuming that there is *one* way to think. It denies the equally powerful logic of correlation and a-causality, the reality of synchronicity and serendipity, and the autonomous thinking capacity of the collective unconscious.

At bottom, we suggest that the engine sustaining the patriarchy's I/it, either/or thinking and behavior is the ancient repression of the feminine principle and the systemic, holistic paradigm it represents. This unconscious process condemns the feminine to the organization shadow and leaves patriarchally dominated organizational hierarchies prone to projecting negatively onto anything *out there* or *in here* that is representative of the feminine or the holistic.

Patriarchally dominated organizations and cultures discriminate against women and scorn the feminine characteristics of nurturing, mentoring, developing, facilitating, connecting, and supporting. In some profound and mysterious way, in the many organizations where the repression of the feminine has occurred, the repressed feminine comes, in the view of the center of consciousness, to be equated with the organization unconscious itself, blinding the patriarchally dominated organization to half of organizational potential.

The repression of the feminine has had the equally disastrous effect of relegating *otherness* in general to the shadow of many organizations. People of color have paid a tragically high price for this in so many organizations. Because people of color have held the shadow for the Caucasian world, many patriarchal leaders (usually white)—at some deep and generally unconscious level—connect the rise of people of color with setting loose aspects of their own unconscious. And since they fear that loosening the bounds of consciousness will allow unconscious material to surface and overrun consciousness, patriarchal leaders have fears about increased organizational diversity (especially at the top).

We believe that it is critical for organizations to break out of this trap laid by the patriarchy, for both the origins of and the solutions to many organizational problems lie in the unconscious regions of organizational culture. Admittedly, getting free is difficult work. But there is potentially a huge pay-off. We believe that with patience, skill, and caring it is possible to help organizations "set aside the bones" of the patriarchy,[2] to move organizations to a level of awareness that allows them to migrate from fearing and feeling threatened by their hidden parts to seeing the interpenetration and inseparability of the conscious and unconscious parts of the organizational system and creating a robust partnership between them.

We know that some people fear that patriarchy would be replaced by its mirror image—matriarchy, a state most people seek to avoid because it reminds them of being an infant in the care of an all-powerful mother figure. What we are suggesting is not about being infantile or dependent. Nor is it about anyone playing second fiddle to anyone else. Cutting-edge management strategies, especially those arising out of system theories and the new sciences, are inherently androgynous, tapping the strengths of *both* the masculine and the feminine poles in a way that creates positive, generative energy.

Understanding and tapping into the organization unconscious requires that organizations work diligently at increasing the diversity of their workforces, creating partnerships between leaders and organizational members, establishing dialogue and consensus as the basis for organizational life, and creating conditions under which everyone—regardless of race, creed, or gender—has a real chance to excel and evolve in the organization. A truly diverse organization membership, broadly invested in the center of consciousness is an organization's best chance for getting to know itself; for engaging in dialogue across the myriad polarities of values, norms, hopes, fears, and expectations that populate any organization; for tapping the full intelligence of the system, which cannot happen when some peoples' views and perspectives are admitted into the consciousness of an organization while others' are not; and for encountering the Archetype of Organization in all its dimensions. Lodged in the collective experience, wisdom, and genes of an organization's members are the seeds of organizational completeness and creativity, as well as the possibility of creating an environment that embraces and supports individuating people instead of seeing them as oddities or threats.

▸ ▸ ▸

Diversity and the Organizational Psyche

Creating and managing a truly diverse workforce is a huge challenge for contemporary organizations. Many organizations have made significant strides toward becoming demographically more diverse and toward protecting the legal rights of their female and nonmajority members. But the next level of diversity work—creating workplaces where every individual can be fully present to the work without being limited by any aspect of his/her uniqueness—has barely begun in most organizations. This is *deep diversity* work, changing an organization's work processes and culture so that the center of consciousness can acknowledge that each organization member is first and foremost unique with respect to his or her soul, the seed of uniqueness planted in each of us at our making.

The absence of a language and a framework for thinking about diversity in this deeper way is a big problem that must be overcome before organizations can move to this next level of diversity work. We have language, laws, and mental models for creating and protecting diversity—primarily the language of ethnic, racial, and gender groups that has powered Equal Employment Opportunity and Affirmative Action efforts (and this work is by no means done!) and inspired multicultural celebrations. But there is no agreed upon language for framing diversity work that takes the uniqueness of each person's soul and the wholeness of the individual as its starting point.

We think that analytical psychology, archetypal psychology, and the beginnings of a Jungian Organization Theory laid out in this book can provide part of a basis for developing the needed framework. Each of these sets of ideas links uniqueness and wholeness—for the individual and the organization, respectively—to the act of allowing the basic life force to flow freely. Each is based on the proposition that psychological health, whether personal or organizational, is rooted in making friends with the shadow, acknowledging and working to integrate the dark side of every individual and organization. In tandem, these sets of ideas offer a language and framework for conceptualizing and talking about how individuated wholeness and *organizational wholeness* can support each other and about how Jung-oriented organizational practitioners can use these ideas to begin moving organizations in the right direction. By articulating the core of personal and organizational meaning, analytical psychology, archetypal psychology, and Jungian Organization Theory point to the place where psychodynamically healthy organizations can celebrate and engage the full energies of unique and individuating organization members.

▸ ▸ ▸

Understanding and tapping into the organization unconscious also requires concepts, blueprints, and road maps. We believe that the organizational psyche model, as well as the other tools and concepts explored in this book, can serve as guides both to analyzing existing psychodynamic processes in organizations and to creating new ones built on healthy dialogue among all voices—conscious and unconscious—in organizations.

THE WISDOM OF BOTH/AND

Entering into this kind of dialogue is a critical first step in what Jung called "hermetic transformation."[3] Hermetic transformation summons up the image of the god Hermes, who unites all the opposites and energizes the inventiveness and the communication of meaning required to bring about change.[4] In organizational terms, hermetic transformation connotes an approach to problem solving and strategy setting in which the legitimate opposing points of view on an issue are identified and held in tension until a course of action that honors both positions and transcends both positions emerges. It is an approach that avoids the sterility of either/or thinking. It hints at a phenomenon Jung called the "*mysterium coniunctionis,* the whole being expressed in the coming together of the opposites."[5] And it opens the door to the "royal marriage"[6] of the four great energy sources flowing through the Archetype of Organization.

Hermetic transformation appears to energize the very core business strategy at the Timberland Company, a New Hampshire-based firm that designs, produces, and distributes specialty footwear, apparel, and accessories. Timberland seems to achieve what often are portrayed as mutually exclusive goals: profitability and good stock market performance on the one hand, and a high level of investment in the community on the other (the company pays its employees, for example, to engage in community service). The company's leaders work at balancing the equation between creating value for the shareholder and creating value for the employee, the consumer, and the community. They self-consciously operate in the tension between Margaret Mead's belief that small groups of concerned individuals can bring about fundamental change and Milton Friedman's assertion that any corporation that gives away money is stealing from its shareholders.[7]

A compelling fictional example of hermetic transformation is presented in the film *Other People's Money*. The container for the process is an aging New England mill that makes wire cable. The polarity is established when Danny DeVito, playing the greedy, unfeeling, Wall Street takeover artist, finds himself confronted in his desire to buy the mill by Gregory Peck, playing the stubborn, tradition-oriented, people-valuing mill owner, who would rather die than sell out his family's legacy. As the story reaches its false ending, neither DeVito's one-sided portrayal of masculine consciousness nor Peck's caricature of feminine unconsciousness has won. DeVito gets the mill but experiences it as one more hollow victory. The stubborn Peck loses his patrimony and faces the likelihood that his actions will threaten the mill's workers with the loss of their livelihood.

The real conclusion, however, is very different. Behind the scenes, the daughter of the mill owner's significant other has moved along a different path. A savvy, feeling, corporate lawyer, she has refused to take an either/or approach and has worked out a sale of the mill by DeVito to a Japanese firm that wants to keep the mill open, but employ the workers in making a different line of products. This ending is emblematic of the kind of transformation that is possible when an organization can identify the polarities inherent in a problem or situation, give them both their due, hold the tension between them, and watch for the emerging solution that yields a glimpse of *organizational wholeness*.

A QUANTUM THEORY OF ORGANIZATION?

Jung set a high standard for using his ideas in the organizational realm. His theory of the individual psyche is elegantly systematic in its insistence that psychic dynamics are all about energy and therefore are ruled by the same laws that govern physical energy; in its insistence that everything is connected to everything else; and in its insistence on the purposeful, self-regulating quality of the psyche. Erich Jantsch, in fact, has suggested that Jung laid down a "quantum theory" of humankind's psychic world.[8] By this, we think Jantsch meant that Jung has given us the concepts and tools needed for understanding human nature at its deepest, most complex, and most mysterious levels.

We believe that it is much easier to understand Jung's theories in the light of contemporary science than in the light of traditional science. Jungian analyst Michael Conforti, for example, suggests that it is best to think about archetypes as fields in which individuals (and we would add, organizations) operate. He links Jungian theory to Ervin Laszlo's work on the psi and vacuum field, Rupert Sheldrake's theory of morphic resonance and formative causation, F. David Peat's work on the interrelationship between mind and matter, David Bohm's concept of implicate order, and Brian Goodwin's and Mae-Wan Ho's work on morphogenetic processes on organisms and fields. Such work, Conforti suggests, helps us understand why people (and, we add, organizations) tend to repeat patterns of behavior even when these patterns are clearly dysfunctional and clearly working counter to the pleasure-principle, by which people and institutions are motivated away from that which causes pain and toward that which gives pleasure.

Our understanding of the mechanics of transformation is similarly explained by the concept of dissipative structures from thermodynamics and chaos theory. In Conforti's words: "On this archetypal level, the repetition creates a thermodynamic dis-equilibrium. At this point in the replicative mode, the human psyche is pushed toward a bifurcation point because of our intrinsic need for growth and meaning making. It has the possibility of utilizing the repetition as a chaotic, rather than a fixed or periodic attractor, thus moving the entire system to a higher level of complexity (negentropy) or of dissolving into endless repetitions."[9]

In organizational terms this means that the field of an archetype may be life-giving unless, in the grip of the complex, it puts the system in a trancelike state in which the pattern defined by the archetype is acted out over and over again against all reason. The patterns recur even when they are operating in a counterproductive way. In this situation, the psychic field operates like a closed system in which the repetition increases entropy.

These repetitions dampen energy and work against the system's desire for vitality and authenticity. Out of the conflict between the forces of life (eros/vitality and meaning) and death (thanatos/entropy and despair) emerges the transcendent function and a realigned organizational psyche, allowing for a truly alchemical transformation. Such a realignment of energies accounts for such seemingly, miraculous events as the fall of the Berlin Wall, the end of apartheid, and a renewed spirit in untold numbers of contemporary organizations. At this point, the organization is suddenly operating at a much higher level of its predominant archetype or even suddenly existing in a different archetypal field altogether.

While it is beyond the boundaries of this book to present in detail the linkages between the new science and a Jungian view of organizational dynamics, suffice it to say that the ideas we offer in this book are fully consistent with quantum and chaos theories. The Jungian Organization Theory that we have begun to spell out points toward a new *cosmology* for understanding the complex adaptive system that is the organization, one that liberates us from the rational, either/or model that has dominated thinking about organizations since the dawn of Newtonian thinking and the industrial age. How to tap this potential for *wholeness* is, we think, one of the great challenges facing organizations and their leaders in this millennium. We believe that Jungian Organization Theory can become a powerful tool for helping organizations *re*-collect and *re*-member the vital unconscious parts of themselves and move toward heretofore unknown levels of internal integration and external adaptiveness.

Notes

1. Capra (1993, in Ray and Rinzler, eds., pp. 230–38).

2. Johnson (1989) inspired this thought. He actually said that individuation starts with the setting aside of the bones of the father—if you can't get past the masculine as interpreted by the father, you remain stuck.

3. McWhinney (1989, p. 192).

4. Bolen (1989, pp. 165–6, 169); Graves (1955, Vol.1, p. 65); and Kerenyi (1988, pp. 164, 247).

5. Jung (C.W. 9, *Part II*, para. 117).

6. See reference to the consummation of the "royal marriage" in Jung (C.W. 5, para. 182).

7. Tyler (1997).

8. Jantsch (1975, p. 174).

9. Conforti (1999, p. 116).

Plotting
YOUR Organization's
Psyche

YOUR Organization's Psyche:
What's There
AND **What's Working?**

If it is possible to do so, take the *Organizational and Team Culture Indicator*™ (with the organization you are going to assess as the reference point) before you start answering the questions in this section. Responses will be even more meaningful if a critical mass of key stakeholders in the organization also takes it, so that you are working from aggregate data. (This protects against the possibility that your individual answers might be biased in some way.)

TASK ONE | **STEP ONE**

We invite you to answer the following questions and plot your answers on worksheet 1 to begin the process of analyzing your organization in a pictorial way. Refer to diagram 1 as needed.

IDENTIFYING THE ORGANIZATION SHADOW

▶ What dynamics and processes are at work in the organization that you have not yet been able to explain to your satisfaction? What confuses or mystifies you?

▶ What values and approaches are *off* limits for discussion for no discernible reason? If, as we argue, these are clues to your organization's shadow, what might you conclude about the contents of that shadow?

▶ When people in your organization complain about people inside or outside the organization, what do they say? Especially note times when those criticisms may seem unfounded to a truly objective third party.

▶ Looking back over the archetypal *human faces* described in chapter 2, what archetypal energies are unacceptable or always interpreted negatively in your organization?

▶ If and when the organization seems to project qualities—negative or positive—onto others so that it is not seeing them or a situation accurately, what qualities are being projected?

▶ In your organization's *OTCI* results, your lowest archetypal Strength scores reflect archetypes that may be missing, be unconscious, or be in the organization's shadow.

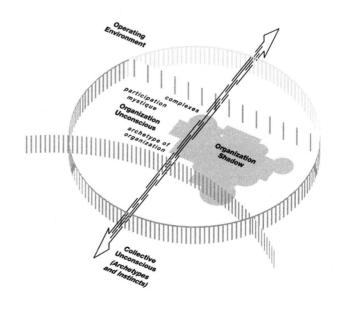

DIAGRAM 1

The Unconscious Organization

IDENTIFYING ORGANIZATIONAL COMPLEXES

▸ Which people in the organization are being "sucked dry" by the roles they are asked to play? What does this tell you about the "participation mystique" and the unconscious pressure people feel to perform in certain ways? How are people *supposed* to act?

▸ Which issues or topics invariably generate high emotion across the organization when they come up? If you could think of these topics and the drama associated with them as being like a movie, play or novel, what would its title be? We might see these behaviors as clues to the complexes at work in your organization. If so, what might you conclude about the nature of those complexes? What might they keep your organization members from seeing clearly?

▸ What is the deep story the organization is living out? Which face of the Archetype of Organization is emphasized by this story? What gifts and threats does this archetypal energy offer?

▸ What are the parts played by various divisions and groups within this larger story? What archetypal configuration results?

WORKSHEET 1
The Unconscious Organization

▸ **ORGANIZATIONAL SHADOW**

▸ **ORGANIZATIONAL COMPLEXES**

TASK ONE | STEP TWO

We invite you to answer the following questions and note your answers on worksheet 2 to continue the process of analyzing your organization in a pictorial way. Refer to and use diagram 2 as needed.

PERSONALIZING THE ARCHETYPE OF ORGANIZATION

▸ With reference to the *OTCI* scores for your organization, mark on worksheet 2 the life energy (*People, Learning, Stabilizing,* or *Results*) that is the highest in your organization. Mark on worksheet 2 the human face of the Archetype of Organization that expresses each quadrant for your organization. Write in the total scores from the *OTCI* results, if you wish, for each human face and each life energy.

▸ With respect to the four life energies—*Learning, Results, People, Stabilizing*—which archetypal face best represents the organization's approach to each?

▸ What is the current balance between these life energies? Is any dangerously high or low?

▸ Which face of the Archetype of Organization best embodies the organization and its reason for being? Which face best embodies the preferred processes of most of the organization's management and employees?

DIAGRAM 2
The Archetype of Organization

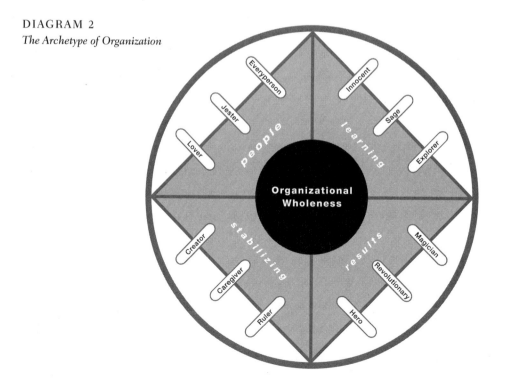

WORKSHEET 2
The Archetype of Organization

▶ **STABILIZING**

_____ Creator

_____ Caregiver

_____ Ruler

▶ **RESULTS**

_____ Revolutionary

_____ Hero

_____ Magician

▶ **PEOPLE**

_____ Jester

_____ Lover

_____ Everyperson

▶ **LEARNING**

_____ Sage

_____ Explorer

_____ Innocent

TASK ONE | **STEP THREE**

We invite you to answer the following questions and note your answers on worksheet 3 to continue the process of analyzing your organization in a pictorial way. Refer to and use diagram 3 as needed.

CENTER OF CONSCIOUSNESS

▸ Where is the locus of power and authority in the organization? Can you envision this group of people as comprising the *ego* of the organization, its center of consciousness? Is this group inclusive enough to make adequate decisions? Does this center of consciousness chart a clear path for the organization? (You might find it interesting to consider everyone left out of this center of consciousness as inhabiting the organization's *unconscious,* with occasional information drifting into the center of consciousness, as with dreams and sudden epiphanies in individuals. If you follow this logic, who is in the unconscious? What do they know that the center of consciousness *does not know?*)

▸ What *typological* characteristics dominate the organizational processes set in motion by the center of consciousness? Put a *plus* by them on worksheet 3. What typological elements are relatively weak or inactive? Put a *minus* by them on the same worksheet.

▸ It may be helpful to have those individuals who are key decision makers take the *Myers-Briggs Type Indicator® (MBTI®)* instrument and create an aggregate chart of results. Then check these results against your assessment of what typological functions the center of consciousness of the organization keeps in its awareness.

▸ What is the relative weight of masculine and feminine energy in day-to-day life in the organization? On worksheet 3, mark the characteristic that predominates. How well developed is the organization in this respect?

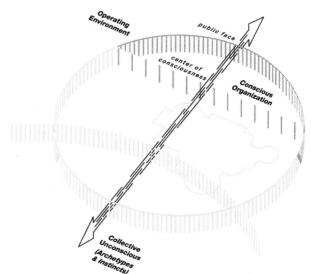

DIAGRAM 3
The Conscious Organization

PUBLIC FACE

‣ How does the organization present itself to the outside world? In what ways does the organization show this public face to its operating environment? Does its brand identity seem to be connected to some archetypal truth about the organization?

‣ Looking back at the *OTCI* scores, if you have them, what archetype would be the best candidate for an archetypal brand identity for the organization? What archetype best embodies the current brand identity of the organization?

WORKSHEET 3
The Conscious Organization

▶ **CENTER OF CONSCIOUSNESS**

___ Extraversion

___ Introversion

___ Sensing

___ Intuition

___ Thinking

___ Feeling

___ Judging

___ Perceiving

___ Masculine

___ Feminine

▶ **PUBLIC FACE**

YOUR
Organization's Psyche:
Pitfalls,
or **What's *Not***
Working?

TASK | **TWO**

We invite you to answer the following questions and note your answers on worksheet 4 to continue the process of analyzing your organization in a pictorial way. Refer to and use diagram 4 as needed.

ZONE 1 AT THE ORGANIZATIONAL BOUNDARY AND BEYOND

‣ How would you describe the organization's brand identity, the conscious dimension of its public face? Is it in sync with the archetypal energies stirring in the organization? Can you see evidence of the unconscious dimension of the organization's public face? Does it "leak" messages from the organization's shadow?

‣ What kind of material is the organization projecting? Onto whom or what is it projecting?

ZONE 2 PROBLEMS AT THE CENTER OF CONSCIOUSNESS

‣ What people, policies, history, or habits are hindering the energy flow in the organization?

‣ Is the center of consciousness well enough developed? Is it invested in enough people? Is it harmfully one-sided?

‣ Does the center of consciousness recognize that the organization has a shadow?

‣ Does the center of conscious understand the organization's complexes?

‣ What is the attitude of the center of consciousness toward developing a relationship with the Archetype of Organization and the collective unconscious?

‣ Is the level of awareness of the center of consciousness appropriate for the organization's life stage?

‣ Is important information sometimes ignored? If so, what are the implications of not facing these facts head on?

ZONE 3 PROBLEMS WITH ORGANIZATIONAL COMPLEXES

‣ Does the organization have any overheated complexes? Are people caught up in a story they compulsively act out?

‣ Are people distorting or failing to see reality clearly? If so, where and about what?

‣ Does the organization seem to need to gobble up people, units, or merged/acquired cultures to protect its way of seeing the world?

ZONE 4 ON THE CUSP OF THE COLLECTIVE UNCONSCIOUS

▸ What aspects of the archetypal realm are welcome in the organization?

▸ Looking back at the unconscious for your organization, what people, archetypal perspectives, typological preferences, and gender styles are relegated to the unconscious of your organization? What would change in your organization if these had a voice?

▸ Of subjects that are off limits, what truth, if it were spoken, would shake up the whole enterprise? Why does no one tell this truth publicly? Where is it spoken privately?

▸ To what extent is this organization open to information coming from dreams, hunches, or feelings in the body? How innovative is the organization?

▸ To what extent is the organization open to benefiting from synchronistic occurrences?

▸ Do you know of breakthroughs that have resulted from such seemingly a-causal coincidences?

DIAGRAM 4
Pitfalls

ZONE 1:
*Problematic Public
Face Projection*

ZONE 2:
*Problematic Center
of Consciousness
Repression
& Denial*

ZONE 3:
*Problematic
Complexes*

ZONE 4:
*Disconnection from
Collective
Unconsciousness*

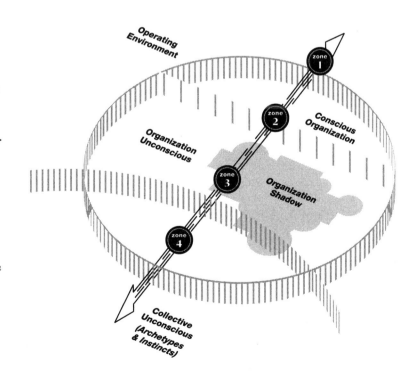

WORKSHEET 4
Pitfalls

▶ **ZONE 1** AT THE
ORGANIZATIONAL
BOUNDARY AND
BEYOND

▶ **ZONE 2** PROBLEMS
AT THE CENTER OF
CONSCIOUSNESS

▶ **ZONE 3** PROBLEMS
WITH ORGANIZATIONAL
COMPLEXES

▶ **ZONE 4** ON THE CUSP
OF THE COLLECTIVE
UNCONSCIOUS

YOUR
Organization's Psyche:
Pathways,
or Moving Toward
Wholeness

TASK | THREE

We invite you to answer the following questions and note your answers on worksheet 5 to continue the process of analyzing your organization in a pictorial way. Refer to and use diagram 5 as needed.

ZONE 1 AT THE ORGANIZATIONAL BOUNDARY AND BEYOND

▸ Which processes of understanding might be appropriate for dealing with concerns about the organization's public face, either the conscious part (the brand identity), or the unconscious part?

▸ What approach would be most useful in identifying the organization's projections, withdrawing them, and learning from them?

ZONE 2 WORKING THE CENTER OF CONSCIOUSNESS

▸ Which processes of understanding might best address issues about the vitality of the center of consciousness?

▸ What interventions would be most helpful in coming to terms with the organization's shadow and integrating the positive energy there into the conscious life of the organization?

ZONE 3 DEALING WITH ORGANIZATIONAL COMPLEXES

▸ Which processes of understanding might be most useful in helping the center of consciousness grapple with over-energized organizational complexes?

ZONE 1:
Strengthening Public Face
Withdrawing Projections

ZONE 2:
Bolstering Center
of Consciousness
Owning the Shadow

ZONE 3:
De-energizing Complexes

ZONE 4:
Dialogue with
the Collective
Unconsciousness

DIAGRAM 5
Pathways

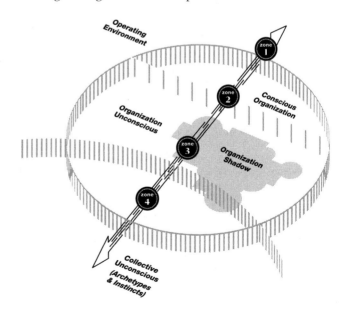

ZONE 4 ON THE CUSP OF THE COLLECTIVE UNCONSCIOUS
  ‣ What positive signs of self-organizing suggest the emergence of energies that signal renewal or life-giving innovation within the organization? What would work best to encourage these developments?

  ‣ Which processes of creative formulation might best be used in helping the center of consciousness begin or continue exploring the archetypal realm?

WORKSHEET 5
Pathways

▌**ZONE 1** AT THE ORGANIZATIONAL BOUNDARY AND BEYOND

▌**ZONE 2** WORKING WITH THE CENTER OF CONSCIOUSNESS

▌**ZONE 3** DEALING WITH ORGANIZATIONAL COMPLEXES

▌**ZONE 4** ON THE CUSP OF THE COLLECTIVE UNCONSCIOUS

Pulling It
All Together

TASK | **FOUR**

We invite you now to lay out for your organization the kind of summary analysis we undertook in chapter 6. Write down the story—the objective, real world data about the organization; think through your Jungian assessment of the situation using the four zones of analysis; and pull together your thoughts about the whole-making processes you think would have the most impact.

▶ **THE STORY:**

_____
_____
_____
_____
_____
_____
_____
_____
_____

▶ **YOUR JUNGIAN ASSESSMENT:**

_____
_____
_____
_____
_____
_____
_____
_____
_____
_____

WHOLE-MAKING PROCESSES:

ADDITIONAL NOTES:

Plotting
a Leader's
Psyche

TASK FIVE | **STEP ONE**

We invite you to answer the following questions and note your answers on worksheet 6. Refer to and use diagram 6 as needed.

PLOTTING YOUR PSYCHE

Identifying Your Shadow

▸ Think about a person who really annoys you or about whom you feel judgmental. What is that person like? What archetypes, type functions, or gender characteristics might be associated with these attitudes and behaviors?

▸ What criticisms do people have of you that seem to you unfounded?

▸ What things do you think or do that seem uncharacteristic, like you were not being yourself?

▸ What do you never want to be like? Of these, which have the most resonance?

▸ In your dreams, what figures seem "other," scary, or transcendent to you?

▸ What is your typological inferior function (the opposite of your dominant function) in *Myers-Briggs Type Indicator (MBTI)* theory? In fact, do you find it difficult to access this function?

Identifying Your Complexes in Both Positive and Negative Guise

▸ What values and what *story* most energize or inspire you?

▸ What novels, films, plays, or real life dramas have helped make you what you are today?

▸ If your life were a movie, what would it be called?

▸ If it is possible, take the *Pearson-Marr Archetype Indicator (PMAI)* instrument. What are your strongest archetypes?

▸ What story *lives you* when you are stressed, feeling compulsive, and out of control?

▸ Notice if there are any kinds of situations you seem always to be experiencing, even though consciously you do not want to have this experience again.

▸ What archetypal story seems to be grabbing you when this happens? (For example, you might want to be laid back, but you find you are attacked again and have to defend yourself.)

▸ If you have recurring dreams, what plot narrative are they acting out?

Identifying the Mandala of the Archetypal Self

▸ With respect to the four life energies—*Learning, Results, People, Stabilizing*—which archetypal face best represents your approach to each?

▸ What does your current balancing of these life energies look like? (Results from the *PMAI*™ instrument, *Archetypal Leadership Styles Survey*™ (appendix C), and *System Stewardship Survey*™ (appendix B) can be helpful here.)

▸ Which human face best embodies the deeper or real you?

▸ When you are the most authentically *you,* what are you like?

▸ When you feel most connected to the world, what are you like?

▸ Looking at the figures in your dreams, and assuming you are all its characters and images, what are the key elements that emerge for you?

▸ If you were to draw a mandala (or even doodle one), what would be the component images?

▸ In what ways is leadership a spiritual pursuit for you?

▸ What practices help you pay attention to your own inner work? What else might you do?

Identifying Your Conscious Qualities or Ego

▸ If you have taken the *MBTI* instrument, what is your *MBTI* type? Beyond your four letter type, what functions work well for you? (For a brief description of the types, see chapter 3 and appendix A.)

▸ What archetypal story do you like to think you are living? What were you taught you should live?

▸ What aspects of femininity and masculinity do you consciously identify with? How masculine, feminine, or androgynous are you in appearance, behavior, and attitudes?

▸ When you walk into an organization, which of the following would naturally grab your attention:

▹ what was being accomplished and how (production subsystem),

▹ how people were relating (human community),

▹ the ideas or learning occurring (learning subsystem), or

▹ the material details, the decor, what people looked like, the procedures you go through in entry (the material system)?

- What might you fail to notice? (Note that the answer to what you ignore may be relevant to the shadow or to an imbalance in the Self in the previous set of questions.)

- What do you believe you should be and do?

- What are your current goals?

Identifying Your Public Image or Persona

- Describe your persona—that is, how do you consciously present yourself to the world?

- What roles do you play in the outer world? Which of them energize you? Which of them drain you?

- What archetype best represents your public image?

DIAGRAM 6
The Leader's Psyche

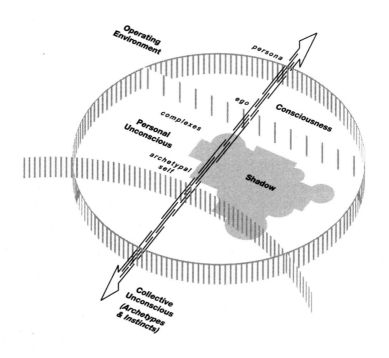

WORKSHEET 6
The Leader's Psyche

▶ **PERSONA**

▶ **EGO**

▶ **SHADOW**

▶ **ARCHETYPAL SELF**

▶ **COMPLEXES**

TASK FIVE | **STEP TWO**

We invite you to answer the following questions and note your answers on worksheets 7a and 7b on pages 144 and 145. Refer to and use diagram 7 as needed.

YOU AND YOUR ORGANIZATION

▸ What are your scores on the *System Stewardship Survey?* On worksheet 7a, circle the life-energy quadrant (*Results, People, Stabilizing, Learning*) where you have the highest score.

▸ What are your scores on the *Archetypal Leadership Styles Survey?* On worksheet 7a, mark the archetypal face that is the strongest for you in each quadrant.

▸ What do your scores on either or both of these instruments tell you about yourself as a leader?

▸ What are you likely to notice and emphasize? What are you likely to ignore, misread, or neglect?

▸ Who on your team might best balance you by seeing what you miss?

▸ How might you help the center of consciousness in your organization recognize the reality of the organization's unconscious parts?

▸ Which of the four subsystems—human, material, productive, learning—in your organization do you pay the most attention to? Put a *plus* by that quadrant on worksheet 7b. Are there any quadrants you ignore? Put a *minus* by them on worksheet 7b. How could you do more to inspirit each of them?

▸ In what capacity do you exert leadership?

▸ As a shepherd of the organization's soul and spirit, how do you tell (and show) the organization's story to all stakeholders in a way that inspires, galvanizes support, and provides a sense of meaning and value to the enterprise? In what way can you honor the organizational legacy, its vision of the future, and what is right about it now?

▸ In steering your organization, what needs to be emphasized in the short term to restore needed balance?

▸ To what degree can you hold the tension between the relative values of *People* versus *Results* or *Learning* versus *Stabilizing?*

▸ Within the human community, how comfortable are you holding the tension when there is conflict between people?

▸ Within the learning subsystem, how comfortable are you holding the tension between conflicting ideas?

▸ Within the material subsystem, how comfortable are you in holding the tension between apparently conflicting policies or practices or between aesthetics and budgetary constraints?

▸ Within the production subsystem, how comfortable are you holding the tension between the need for efficiency and speed and the need for quality controls?

▸ What strategies might you use to avoid premature closure that forecloses the emergence of the transcendent function in each of these areas?

▸ In comparing the map of your psyche with the maps of your organization, what do you notice?

▸ How are you like your organization? How are you different? How might the differences and similarities enhance or undermine you leadership efforts?

DIAGRAM 7
Organizational Subsystems:
Energized by the Archetype of Organization

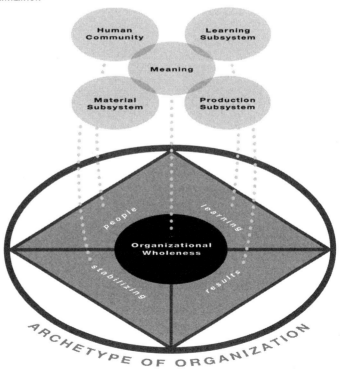

WORKSHEET 7a
The Leader's Psyche

▶ **STABILIZING**

___ Creator

___ Caregiver

___ Ruler

▶ **RESULTS**

___ Revolutionary

___ Hero

___ Magician

▶ **PEOPLE**

___ Jester

___ Lover

___ Everyperson

▶ **LEARNING**

___ Sage

___ Explorer

___ Innocent

WORKSHEET 7b
The Leader's Psyche

▶ **MATERIAL SUBSYSTEM**

▶ **PRODUCTION SUBSYSTEM**

▶ **HUMAN COMMUNITY**

▶ **LEARNING SUBSYSTEM**

TASK FIVE | **STEP THREE**

We invite you now to set down for yourself a narrative summary of the analysis you have just completed in Task Five/Steps One and Two. Write down your story (who you are as a person and leader described in everyday language); think through your Jungian assessment of yourself and your relationship to the organization you have been assessing throughout this book; and pull together your thoughts about whole-making processes that would make you a more complete person and leader.

▶ THE STORY:

▶ YOUR JUNGIAN ASSESSMENT:

WHOLE-MAKING PROCESSES:

ADDITIONAL NOTES:

Plotting
a Consultant's
Psyche

TASK SIX | **STEP ONE**

We invite you to answer the following questions and note your answers on worksheet 8 on pages 154 and 155. Refer to and use diagram 8 as needed. (These questions pertain primarily to consultants. However it is also possible for a leader or employee at any level of an organization to sometimes think about the organization and its issues in the way a consultant would. To do this, it is important to take the role of the outsider or to honor the ways you do not completely fit in. Although those ways may seem a hindrance to belonging, they also provide you with the perspective to see at least some aspects of organizational practice from outside. If you already did an individual analysis in completing task five/step one, refer back to those data at this point rather than going on with this task.)

MAPPING YOUR PSYCHE

Identifying Your Shadow

▸ Think about a person who really annoys you or about whom you feel judgmental. What is that person like? What archetypes or type functions or gender characteristics might be associated with these attitudes and behaviors?

▸ What criticisms do people have of you that seem to you unfounded?

▸ What things do you think or do that seem uncharacteristic, like you were not being yourself?

▸ What do you never want to be like? Of these, which have the most resonance?

▸ In your dreams, what figures seem "other," scary, or transcendent to you?

▸ What is your typological inferior function (the opposite of your dominant function) in *Myers-Briggs Type Indicator (MBTI)* theory? In fact, do you find it difficult to access this function?

Identifying Your Complexes in Both Positive and Negative Guise

▸ What values and what story most energize or inspire you?

▸ What novels, films, plays, or real life dramas have helped make you what you are today?

▸ If your life were a movie, what would it be called?

▸ If it is possible, take the *Pearson-Marr Archetype Indicator (PMAI)* instrument. What are your strongest archetypes?

▸ What story lives you when you are stressed, feeling compulsive, and out of control?

▸ Notice if there are any kinds of situations you seem always to be experiencing, even though consciously you do not want to have this experience again.

▸ What archetypal story seems to be grabbing you when this happens? (For example, you might want to be laid back, but you find you are attacked again and have to defend yourself.)

▸ If you have recurring dreams, what plot narrative are they acting out?

Identifying the Mandala of the Archetypal Self

▸ With respect to the four life energies—*Learning, Results, People, Stabilizing*—which archetypal face best represents your approach to each?

▸ What is your current balancing on these life energies? (*PMAI* results can be helpful here.)

▸ Which archetype best embodies the deeper or real you?

▸ When you are the most authentically *you,* what are you like?

▸ When you feel most connected to the world, what are you like?

▸ Looking at the figures in your dreams, and assuming you are all its characters and images, what are the key elements that emerge for you?

▸ If you were to draw a mandala (or even doodle one), what would be the component images?

▸ In what ways is leadership a spiritual pursuit for you?

▸ What practices help you pay attention to your own inner work? What else might you do?

Identifying Your Conscious Qualities or Ego

▸ If you have taken the *Myers-Briggs Type Indicator* instrument, what is your *MBTI* type? Beyond your four letter type, what functions work well for you?

▸ What archetypal story do you like to think you are living? What story were you taught you should live?

▸ What aspects of femininity and masculinity do you consciously identify with? How masculine, feminine, or androgynous are you in appearance, behavior, and attitudes?

▸ When you walk into an organization, which of the following would naturally grab your attention:

▷ what was being accomplished and how (production subsystem),

▷ how people were relating (community),

▷ the ideas or learning occurring (learning subsystem)

▷ or the material details, the decor, what people looked like, the procedures you go through in entry (the material system)?

▸ What might you fail to notice? (Note that the answer to what you *ignore* may be relevant to the shadow or to an imbalance in the Self above).

▸ What do you believe you should be and do?

▸ What are your current goals?

Identifying Your Public Image or Persona

▸ Describe your persona—that is, how do you consciously present yourself to the world?

▸ What roles do you play in the outer world? Which of them energize you? Drain you?

▸ What archetype best represents your public image?

YOU AND YOUR CLIENT ORGANIZATION

▸ Is the center of consciousness ready for and open to encountering the organization's unconscious "stuff"? If it is not ready, what can you do to prepare it?

▸ Is your relationship with the organization one of partnership? If not, could it become that?

▸ Are you aware of any ways in which your own unconscious material has gotten in the way of sustaining a healthy relationship with the organization? How do you feel when you are involved in this organization? What story does it feel like you are in? What role in it are you playing? What does this tell you about yourself? What does this tell you about the organization? In what ways you are personally wounded? What part of your story is appropriate to raise in this consulting relationship?

▸ What makes you care about this organization? Can you bring love to your work with this organization?

▸ What do you see in the organization that does not appear to be clear to others?

▸ What are some ways that you are, or could become, a catalyst for change?

▸ How do you, or might you, serve as a container that promotes safety and sacred, healing space in the organization?

▸ Who are you with this client?

▸ What is on the pages of your own "soul book" for working with organizations from a Jungian perspective? What ideas about organizational whole-making are beginning to tickle the corners of your mind?

▸ In comparing the map of your psyche with the maps of your client organization, what opportunities and potential dangers can you recognize? What inner work might you need to undertake to work more successfully with this client? How might you expect to be changed in the interaction?

DIAGRAM 8
The Consultant's Psyche

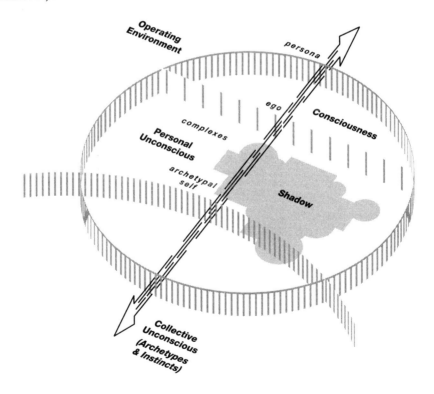

WORKSHEET 8
The Consultant's Psyche

◗ **COMPLEXES**

◗ **PERSONA**

◗ **EGO**

▶ **SHADOW**

▶ **ARCHETYPAL SELF**

TASK SIX | **STEP TWO**

We invite you now to set down for yourself a narrative summary of the analysis you have just completed in Task Six/Step One. Write down your story (who you are as a person and consultant described in everyday language); think through your Jungian assessment of yourself and your relationship to the organization you have been assessing throughout this book; and pull together your thoughts about whole-making processes that would make you a more complete person and consultant.

◗ **THE STORY:**

◗ **YOUR JUNGIAN ASSESSMENT:**

WHOLE-MAKING PROCESSES:

ADDITIONAL NOTES:

MBTI®
Type
Descriptions

ISTJ

For ISTJs the dominant quality in their lives is an abiding sense of responsibility for doing what needs to be done in the here-and-now. Their realism, organizing abilities, and command of the facts lead to their completing tasks thoroughly and with great attention to detail. Logical pragmatists at heart, ISTJs make decisions based on their experience and with an eye to efficiency in all things. ISTJs are intensely committed to people and to the organizations of which they are a part; they take their work seriously and believe others should do so as well.

ISFJ

For ISFJs the dominant quality in their lives is an abiding respect and sense of personal responsibility for doing what needs to be done in the here-and-now. Actions that are of practical help to others are of particular importance to ISFJs. Their realism, organizing abilities, and command of the facts lead to their thorough attention in completing tasks. ISFJs bring an aura of quiet warmth, caring, and dependability to all that they do; they take their work seriously and believe others should do so as well.

ISTP

For ISTPs the driving force in their lives is to understand how things and phenomena in the real world work so they can make the best and most effective use of them. They are logical and realistic people, and they are natural troubleshooters. When not actively solving a problem, ISTPs are quiet and analytical observers of their environment, and they naturally look for the underlying sense to any facts they have gathered. ISTPs often pursue variety and even excitement in their hands-on experiences. Although they do have a spontaneous, even playful side, what people often first encounter with them is their detached pragmatism.

ISFP

For ISFPs the dominant quality in their lives is a deep-felt caring for living things, combined with a quietly playful and sometimes adventurous approach to life and all its experiences. ISFPs typically show their caring in very practical ways, since they often prefer action to words. Their warmth and concern are generally not expressed openly, and what people often first encounter with ISFPs is their quiet adaptability, realism, and "free spirit" spontaneity.

ESTP

For ESTPs the dominant quality in their lives is their enthusiastic attention to the outer world of hands-on and real-life experiences. ESTPs are excited by continuous involvement in new activities and in the pursuit of new challenges. They tend to be logical and analytical in their approach to life, and they have an acute sense of how objects, events, and people in the world work. ESTPs are typically energetic and adaptable realists, who prefer to experience and accept life rather than to judge or organize it.

ESFP

For ESFPs the dominant quality in their lives is their enthusiastic attention to the outer world of hands-on and real-life experiences. ESFPs are excited by continuous involvement in new activities and new relationships. They also have a deep concern for people, and they show their caring in warm and pragmatic gestures of helping. ESFPs are typically energetic and adaptable realists, who prefer to experience and accept life rather than to judge or organize it.

ESTJ

For ESTJs the driving force in their lives is their need to analyze and bring into logical order the outer world of events, people, and things. ESTJs like to organize anything that comes into their domain, and they will work energetically to complete tasks so they can quickly move from one to the next. Sensing orients their thinking to current facts and realities, and thus gives their thinking a pragmatic quality. ESTJs take their responsibilities seriously and believe others should do so as well.

ESFJ

For ESFJs the dominant quality in their lives is an active and intense caring about people and a strong desire to bring harmony into their relationships. ESFJs bring an aura of warmth to all that they do, and they naturally move into action to help others, to organize the world around them, and to get things done. Sensing orients their feeling to current facts and realities, and thus gives their feeling a hands-on pragmatic quality. ESFJs take their work seriously and believe others should do so as well.

Excerpted from *Building People Building Programs* by Gordon Lawrence and Charles Martin (CAPT 2001).

INFJ

For INFJs the dominant quality in their lives is their attention to the inner world of possibilities, ideas, and symbols. Knowing by way of insight is paramount for them, and they often manifest a deep concern for people and relationships as well. INFJs often have deep interests in creative expression as well as issues of spirituality and human development. While their energy and attention are naturally drawn to the inner world of ideas and insights, what people often first encounter with INFJs is their drive for closure and for the application of their ideas to people's concerns.

INFP

For INFPs the dominant quality in their lives is a deep-felt caring and idealism about people. They experience this intense caring most often in their relationships with others, but they may also experience it around ideas, projects, or any involvement they see as important. INFPs are often skilled communicators, and they are naturally drawn to ideas that embody a concern for human potential. INFPs live in the inner world of values and ideals, but what people often first encounter with them in the outer world is their adaptability and concern for possibilities.

ENFP

For ENFPs the dominant quality in their lives is their attention to the outer world of possibilities; they are excited by continuous involvement in anything new, whether it be new ideas, new people, or new activities. Though ENFPs thrive on what is possible and what is new, they also experience a deep concern for people as well. Thus, they are especially interested in possibilities for people. ENFPs are typically energetic, enthusiastic people who lead spontaneous and adaptable lives.

ENFJ

For ENFJs the dominant quality in their lives is an active and intense caring about people and a strong desire to bring harmony into their relationships. ENFJs are openly expressive and empathic people who bring an aura of warmth to all that they do. Intuition orients their feeling to the new and to the possible, thus they often enjoy working to manifest a humanitarian vision or helping others develop their potential. ENFJs naturally and conscientiously move into action to care for others, to organize the world around them, and to get things done.

INTJ

For INTJs the dominant force in their lives is their attention to the inner world of possibilities, symbols, abstractions, images, and thoughts. Insight in conjunction with logical analysis is the essence of their approach to the world; they think systemically. Ideas are the substance of life for INTJs and they have a driving need to understand, to know, and to demonstrate competence in their areas of interest. INTJs inherently trust their insights, and with their task-orientation will work intensely to make their visions into realities.

INTP

For INTPs the driving force in their lives is to understand whatever phenomenon is the focus of their attention. They want to make sense of the world—as a concept—and they often enjoy opportunities to be creative. INTPs are logical, analytical, and detached in their approach to the world; they naturally question and critique ideas and events as they strive for understanding. INTPs usually have little need to control the outer world, or to bring order to it, and they often appear very flexible and adaptable in their lifestyle.

ENTP

For ENTPs the dominant quality in their lives is their attention to the outer world of possibilities; they are excited by continuous involvement in anything new, whether it be new ideas, new people, or new activities. They look for patterns and meaning in the world, and they often have a deep need to analyze, to understand, and to know the nature of things. ENTPs are typically energetic, enthusiastic people who lead spontaneous and adaptable lives.

ENTJ

For ENTJs the driving force in their lives is their need to analyze and bring into logical order the outer world of events, people, and things. ENTJs are natural leaders who build conceptual models that serve as plans for strategic action. Intuition orients their thinking to the future and gives their thinking an abstract quality. ENTJs will actively pursue and direct others in the pursuit of goals they have set, and they prefer a world that is structured and organized.

System
Stewardship
SURVEY™

This section contains the complete System Stewardship Survey™ referred to in chapters 5, 6, and 7. The thirty-six-item, self-scoring survey comes first, followed by a scoring guide, a diagram for plotting scores, some technical information about the survey, and a few interpretative suggestions.

PART I

Using the following ranking, write a 1, 2, 3, 4, or 5 in the space before each item:

     1—I never do this.

     2—I rarely do this

     3—I sometimes do this.

     4—I do this quite often

     5—I do this regularly

_____1. Make sure that the organization's outputs meet the customer's needs (quality, timeliness).

_____2. Play a linking role between units and processes in the organization.

_____3. Focus on building the organization's capacity for success in the future.

_____4. Work to develop the skills and abilities of organization members.

_____5. Utilize the organization's resources efficiently.

_____6. Provide stability in the midst of change.

_____7. Demonstrate multi-perspective thinking.

_____8. Foster the effectiveness and growth of work units.

_____9. Make sure that everything the organization does relates to its purpose for existing.

_____10. Sort out competing priorities.

_____11. See the organization as a whole.

_____12. Ensure that appropriate organizational resources (time, money) are focused on developing human capital.

_____13. Effectively direct the work, delegating authority to organization members as appropriate.

_____14. Remind the organization of its roots and enduring values.

_____15. Solicit feedback from inside *and* outside the organization and use it as appropriate to change direction or priorities.

_____16. Show sensitivity to work and family issues.

_____17. Help organization members understand how their work relates to the purposes of the larger organization.

_____18. Monitor spending and stay within budgets.

_____19. Create partnerships with key players outside the organization to get the job done.

_____20. Strive for solutions to personnel issues that meet the individual's needs and the organization's needs.

_____21. Set organizational priorities.

_____22. Hold organization members accountable for using organizational resources appropriately.

_____23. Demonstrate a bias for continuous improvement.

_____24. Respect the uniqueness and dignity of all organization members.

_____25. Link rewards to organizational goals.

_____26. Articulate ethical standards.

_____27. Know how to work the system to get things done.

_____28. Demonstrate an understanding of the impossibility of doing more with less.

_____29. Get the work out the door.

_____30. Show skill in the creation and use of management information systems.

_____31. Garner the resources necessary for doing the job.

_____32. Recognize that communication is about more than just information, that organization members need to be able to give voice to feelings and values, as well.

___33. Do whatever it takes.

___34. Create an appropriate balance among the organization's systems, work processes, structure, and culture.

___35. Discourage the "not invented here" syndrome.

___36. Strive to establish the organization as an "employer of choice."

PART II

Next, transfer your score for each item to the following chart and do the math as directed:

Results

_____1. Make sure that the organization's outputs meet the customer's needs (quality, timeliness).

_____5. Utilize the organization's resources efficiently.

_____9. Make sure that everything the organization does relates to its purpose for existing.

___13. Effectively direct the work, delegating authority to organization members as appropriate.

___17. Help organization members understand how their work relates to the purposes of the larger organization.

___21. Set organizational priorities.

___25. Link rewards to organizational goals.

___29. Get the work out the door.

___33. Do whatever it takes.

_____ **Total *points* for Results**

_____ **Score for Results** (*Divide total points by 9*)

Stabilizing

_____2. Play a linking role between units and processes in the organization.

_____6. Provide stability in the midst of change.

___10. Sort out competing priorities.

___14. Remind the organization of its roots and enduring values.

___18. Monitor spending and stay within budgets.

___22. Hold organization members accountable for using organizational resources appropriately.

____26. Articulate ethical standards.

____30. Show skill in the creation and use of management information systems.

____34. Create an appropriate balance among the organization's systems, work processes, structure, and culture.

   ____ **Total *points* for Stabilizing**

   ____ **Score for Stabilizing** (*Divide total points by 9*))

Learning

____3. Focus on building the organization's capacity for success in the future.

____7. Demonstrate multiperspective thinking.

____11. See the organization as a whole.

____15. Solicit feedback from inside and outside the organization and use it as appropriate to change direction or priorities.

____19. Create partnerships with key players outside the organization to get the job done.

____23. Demonstrate a bias for continuous improvement.

____27. Know how to work the system to get things done.

____31. Garner the resources necessary for doing the job.

____35. Discourage the "not invented here" syndrome.

   ____**Total *points* for Learning**

   ____**Score for Learning** (*Divide total points by 9*)

People

____4. Work to develop the skills and abilities of organization members.

____8. Foster the effectiveness and growth of work units.

____12. Ensure that appropriate organizational resources (time, money) are focused on developing human capital.

____16. Show sensitivity to work-family issues.

____20. Strive for solutions to personnel issues that meet the individual's needs and the organization's needs.

____24. Respect the uniqueness and dignity of all organization members.

____28. Demonstrate an understanding of the impossibility of doing more with less.

____32. Recognize that communication is about more than just information . . . that organization members need to be able to give voice to feelings and values, as well.

____36. Strive to establish the organization as an "employer of choice."

    ____**Total** *points* **for People**

    ____**Score for People** (*Divide total points by 9*)

PART III.

Transfer your four scores to the following chart:

<table>
<tr>
<td align="center">_____
Your Score</td>
<td></td>
<td align="center">_____
Your Score</td>
</tr>
<tr>
<td align="center">

People

</td>
<td></td>
<td align="center">

Learning

</td>
</tr>
</table>

Creative Tension of Leadership

<table>
<tr>
<td align="center">_____
Your Score</td>
<td></td>
<td align="center">_____
Your Score</td>
</tr>
<tr>
<td align="center">

Stabilizing

</td>
<td></td>
<td align="center">

Results

</td>
</tr>
</table>

INFORMATION ABOUT THE *SYSTEM STEWARDSHIP SURVEY*

▶ The *System Stewardship Survey* is *not* a finely honed psychometric instrument. There are no statistically significant or insignificant results.

▶ However, based on several years of use with managerial leaders, the *Survey* seems to be a broadly reliable indicator of possible strengths and weaknesses in your approach to managerial leadership.

▶ The highest possible score in each of the four categories of leadership behavior is "5."

▶ If you're human (and honest with yourself) you're not likely to score all "5s."

INTERPRETING YOUR *SYSTEM STEWARDSHIP* SCORES

▶ Each of the four system quadrants represents a vital aspect of a healthy organization's life. *Results* stands for all the activities involved with getting products and services out the door. *People* stands for the work of growing and developing human capital. *Stabilizing* stands for the support processes surrounding the core production work of the organization. *Learning* stands for the growth, change, and adaptation that characterize any healthy organization.

▶ The exigencies of the workplace may require the managerial leader to focus for a time on one or another of the quadrants to the exclusion of the others. However, over time, each quadrant requires the attention of the managerial leader if the organization is to be truly effective.

▶ Each of the four system quadrants is energized by the dimension of the Archetype of Organization bearing the same name.

▶ The *Survey* is designed to give you a sense of the relative degree of attention you give to each of the four quadrants, as well as the main archetypal energies you are tapping into during the course of carrying out your leadership responsibilities.

▶ Practice suggests that a rough balance in your scores at the "3.5–4" level is the most desirable profile, suggesting that you are holding all the critical organizational processes in creative tension with each other and that you are in adequate touch with all four of the life energies of the Archetype of Organization.

▶ If you have scores below "3" in one or two areas, you may want to consider the possibility that you have some cognitive or emotional blind spots that are negatively affecting your ability to be a good steward of your organization. Success as a managerial leader ultimately lies in transcending any such biases and managing the organizational system as a whole.

Archetypal
Leadership Styles
Survey™

The survey may be taken by a leader as a self-report. It can also be used as a 360-degree-feedback tool and filled out by people over, under, and around the leader. If the reader is not the leader and is not in a position to recruit the leader to take the instrument (as a self-assessment or a 360-degree-feedback tool), you can rate the leader yourself for the purpose of understanding and reviewing the exercises in this book.

As you work through the survey, remember that *product* includes products, services, messages, etc., and *customer* includes customers, clients, patients, students, members, constituents, audience, public, etc.

INSTRUCTIONS

Place the name of that leader (yourself or another) in the blank provided at the beginning of the chart. Put a check mark in the box by each phrase below that describes the leader you are assessing. After you have completed the survey (pages 170–176), turn to the scoring grid on page 177 and fill in the scores. Then turn to page 178 and complete the information to assess your scores.

NOTE ABOUT SCORING

Rather than calculating your scores, you may wish to just note the archetypal categories where the check marks congregate and get an overall impression of the archetypal influences.

ARCHETYPAL LEADERSHIP STYLES SURVEY

Leader's Name:_____

Innocent

Values

- ☐ loyalty
- ☐ people who follow the rules
- ☐ tried and true policies
- ☐ personal character

Is good at

- ☐ providing clear guidelines to employees
- ☐ offering employees long-term security
- ☐ training employees to do things right
- ☐ taking care of employees

Finds it difficult to

- ☐ encourage innovation
- ☐ deal with employees who rock the boat
- ☐ face problems until they escalate
- ☐ grapple with complex problems

Explorer

Values

- ☐ independence
- ☐ self-starters
- ☐ pioneers
- ☐ authenticity

Is good at

- ☐ supporting employee autonomy
- ☐ discouraging conformist thinking
- ☐ minimizing bureaucracy
- ☐ seeking out new ideas and perspectives

Finds it difficult to

☐ coordinate activities

☐ be a team player

☐ keep everyone informed

☐ pay enough attention to staff to supervise them adequately

Sage

Values

☐ knowledge

☐ expertise

☐ quality results

☐ a learning community

Is good at

☐ fostering continuous learning

☐ putting evaluation processes in place

☐ research and development

☐ analyzing complex issues

Finds it difficult to

☐ deal with people who do not seem very bright

☐ act until all the facts are in and analyzed

☐ see through someone who sounds intelligent but is off track

☐ anticipate people's feeling responses

Hero

Values

☐ a can-do spirit

☐ people who consistently come through (no excuses)

☐ achieving goals

☐ the toughness to get the job done

Is good at

- ☐ getting things done
- ☐ creating clear goals and outcomes
- ☐ motivating people to work very hard
- ☐ coaching the team on how to succeed

Finds it difficult to

- ☐ walk away from a challenge
- ☐ slow down and re-evaluate
- ☐ respect the perspective of someone who disagrees with him/her/you
- ☐ sympathize with anyone who seems like a loser

Revolutionary

Values

- ☐ cutting-edge ideas and practices
- ☐ radically innovative change
- ☐ a critical spirit
- ☐ people who continually question how things are done

Is good at

- ☐ rethinking outmoded practices
- ☐ taking risks
- ☐ considering people's wilder ideas
- ☐ radical innovation

Finds it difficult to

- ☐ stick to established practices
- ☐ keep his/her/your mouth shut
- ☐ get along with conventional people
- ☐ learn from the past

Magician

Values

- [ ] self-awareness
- [ ] win/win solutions
- [ ] seemingly miraculous outcomes
- [ ] catalysts for change

Is good at

- [ ] reframing problems as opportunities
- [ ] being charismatic
- [ ] vision clarification
- [ ] allowing flexibility in how groups accomplish goals

Finds it difficult to

- [ ] recognize that a miracle may not pull things out at the last moment
- [ ] limit aspirations
- [ ] distinguish a flaky idea from a sound one
- [ ] keep on top of everything that is going on

Everyperson

Values

- [ ] the dignity of the common man or woman
- [ ] employees who are solid and unpretentious
- [ ] banding together to survive tough times
- [ ] a good day's work for a day's pay

Is good at

- [ ] rewarding employees who try
- [ ] treating everyone equally
- [ ] implementing fair employment policies
- [ ] being empathic with employees

Finds it difficult to

☐ provide advancement opportunities

☐ provide many amenities or perks

☐ require people to work hard and effectively

☐ deal with anyone who seems to think they are special

Lover

Values

☐ emotional intelligence

☐ personal attractiveness

☐ a sense of community

☐ consensual decision making

Is good at

☐ fostering a sense of real caring among employees

☐ treating each employee as special

☐ building positive relationships with customers

☐ getting everyone's input on decisions

Finds it difficult to

☐ separate the personal from the professional

☐ deal with conflict

☐ take an unpopular stand

☐ respect other people's rights to privacy

Jester

Values

☐ ways to make work fun

☐ playful inventiveness

☐ humor

☐ seeing clever ways around obstacles

Is good at

- ☐ brainstorming
- ☐ lightening people up
- ☐ making work fun
- ☐ allowing flexible work schedules

Finds it difficult to

- ☐ plan ahead
- ☐ get paper work done
- ☐ do boring work
- ☐ resist making a joke at someone's expense

Caregiver

Values

- ☐ people who show care for others
- ☐ sacrificing for the greater good
- ☐ being of service
- ☐ helping those most in need

Is good at

- ☐ caring for others
- ☐ customer service
- ☐ inspiring employees to be caring to one another
- ☐ providing a warm, nurturing environment

Finds it difficult to

- ☐ say no to anyone in need
- ☐ assess the cost to the staff before making commitments
- ☐ require others to be as self-reliant as possible
- ☐ know his/her/your own limits

Creator

Values

☐ creative endeavors

☐ imaginative products

☐ self-expression

☐ good (aesthetic) taste

Is good at

☐ fostering creative teams

☐ encouraging innovative products

☐ allowing employees the freedom to be imaginative

☐ taking an imaginative approach to life and work

Finds it difficult to

☐ focus on noncreative activities

☐ limit innovation to what can be produced and marketed

☐ say no to a promising idea

☐ refrain from prima-donna behaviors

Ruler

Values

☐ providing the standard others will follow

☐ political savvy

☐ prestige and power

☐ knowing the inside scoop on how to get things done

Is good at

☐ fostering clear lines of authority

☐ being a strong leader

☐ conferring status by association

☐ putting systems in place to ensure timely and quality results

Finds it difficult to

☐ resist creating overly complex bureaucratic processes

☐ deal fairly with people who challenge your/his/her authority

☐ sacrifice image to results

☐ tear him/her/yourself away from office politics to get the work done

SCORING SHEET

Innocent
____ Values
____ Strengths (Is good at)
____ Challenges (Finds it difficult to)
    _____Total

Explorer
____ Values
____ Strengths (Is good at)
____ Challenges (Finds it difficult to)
    _____Total

Sage
____ Values
____ Strengths (Is good at)
____ Challenges (Finds it difficult to)
    _____Total

Hero
____ Values
____ Strengths (Is good at)
____ Challenges (Finds it difficult to)
    _____Total

Revolutionary
____ Values
____ Strengths (Is good at)
____ Challenges (Finds it difficult to)
    _____Total

Magician
____ Values
____ Strengths (Is good at)
____ Challenges (Finds it difficult to)
    _____Total

Everyperson
____ Values
____ Strengths (Is good at)
____ Challenges (Finds it difficult to)
    _____Total

Lover
____ Values
____ Strengths (Is good at)
____ Challenges (Finds it difficult to)
    _____Total

Jester
____ Values
____ Strengths (Is good at)
____ Challenges (Finds it difficult to)
    _____Total

Caregiver
____ Values
____ Strengths (Is good at)
____ Challenges (Finds it difficult to)
    _____Total

Creator
____ Values
____ Strengths (Is good at)
____ Challenges (Finds it difficult to)
    _____Total

Ruler
____ Values
____ Strengths (Is good at)
____ Challenges (Finds it difficult to)
    _____Total

ASSESSMENT SHEET

List the archetypes with the highest Total scores:

Highest _____

Second highest _____

Third highest _____

List the archetypes with the highest Values scores:

Highest _____

Second Highest _____

Third Highest _____

List the archetypes with the highest Strengths scores (Is good at):

Highest _____

Second Highest _____

Third Highest _____

List the archetypes with the highest Challenges scores (Finds it difficult to):

Highest _____

Second Highest _____

Third Highest _____

NOTES

_____

_____

_____

_____

_____

_____

Archetypes
OF Family
Culture™

The chart on the following pages will help you determine the archetype most like your family of origin. You can use this information to help you understand what "story" you may be projecting onto organizations. If your family of origin was quite complex, you may wish to select a number of archetypes.

Use the space below to summarize your thoughts regarding your family of origin's archetypes. *My family of origin was living out the following story (or stories):*

_____

_____

_____

_____

_____

_____

_____

_____

Archetype	Image	Virtues Fostered	Likely Wounds	Injunction
Innocent	Stereotypical happy family; everyone cheerful, helpful, being "perfect."	Cheerfulness Trustworthiness Optimism Simple goodness	Denial Superficiality Naiveté Childishness	Be good. Follow the rules.
Orphan/ Everyperson	Overwhelmed or salt-of-the-earth parents just getting by and kids having to cope.	Resilience Realism Adaptability Humility Empathy	Low expectations Cynicism Feeling orphaned Victim mentality	Be realistic. Make the best from what you can have.
Caregiver	Altruistic parents, helping the world, and teaching children to share and nurture others.	Compassion Altruism Unselfishness Sympathy	Martyr behaviors Weak boundaries Co-dependence	Be kind. Help those in need.
Warrior/ Hero	Parents as coaches, encouraging achievement and winning.	Discipline Courage Assertiveness Ambition	Workaholism Ruthlessness Stoicism Burnout	Be strong. Fight for what you want (or what you believe in).
Seeker/ Explorer	Independent parents fostering autonomy; everyone going their own way.	Independence Adventurousness Self-reliance Ability to follow one's own star	Loneliness Perfectionism Aimless wandering Loner	Be authentic. Find yourself and your path.
Destroyer/ Revolutionary	Family in midst of trauma—severe loss of some kind; counterculture family.	Ability to reinvent self Early maturity Risk taking Out-of-the-box thinking	Feeling different Fear of life Escape to spiritual or psychic reality Disrespect Antisocial attitudes	Be daring. When things are not working try something new

Archetype	Image	Virtues Fostered	Likely Wounds	Injunction
Lover	Close family with much touching, interaction, emotional sharing, and beauty.	Intimacy skills Passion Love Sensuality	Conflict avoidance Boundary confusion Loss of individuality	Be close. Love is what you need.
Creator	Artistic, imaginative family encouraging self-expression.	Creativity Expressiveness Authenticity Ability to imagine	Eccentricity Prima donna attitudes Difficulty with routine	Be creative. Express yourself.
Ruler	Like a royal family with much focus on protocol and being examples to others.	Self-assurance Responsibility Decorum Knowing how things are done	Elitism Entitlement Fear of exile Dictatorial behaviors	Take command. Always be in control.
Magician	Like magic circle of wizards searching out secrets of the universe.	Vision Ability to work with synergy and synchronicity Self-awareness	Manipulative behaviors Marginality Cultishness Impracticality	Be conscious. Be the future you wish for.
Sage	Intellectual family engaged in furthering the life of the mind.	Curiosity Rationality Objectivity Intelligence	Inability to act Judgmentalism Dogmatism Living in the head	Be smart. Think for yourself.
Jester	A family that loves to play and have fun; life as a game.	Lightness Cleverness Capacity for enjoyment Being in the moment	Irresponsibility Debauchery Drifting through life Failure to take self seriously	Be fun. Life is for living.

Glossary

active imagination. Various techniques used in Jungian analysis to dialogue with unconscious material. The methods include verbal (e.g., imaginary conversation with a figure from the unconscious) and non-verbal (e.g., drawing).

analytical psychology. The psychological theory and praxis of the Swiss psychologist C. G. Jung. See depth psychology.

anima/animus. Anima is the archetype of what, for the human male, is the totally other, his feminine quality. Animus is the archetype of what, for the human female, is the totally other, her masculine quality.

archetype. A typical, uniform, and regularly recurring mode of perception. It is a psychological predisposition to an image that underlies human behavior. The domain of the archetype is the collective unconscious.

Archetype of Organization. The rough organizational analogy of the archetypal Self. The dominant, or centrally constellated, archetype of the organizational psyche.

archetypal psychology. A school of psychology which asserts that archetypal theory is the most fundamental area of Jung's work, but that this was not obvious when Jung coined the term analytical psychology.

archetypal Self. See Self.

attitude. The psyche's orientation toward psychic energy. The extraverted attitude is characterized by a flow of psychic energy toward the outer world of people and objects. The introverted attitude is characterized by a flow of psychic energy toward the inner world of ideas and reflection. See psychological types.

center of consciousness. The rough analogy in the organizational psyche for the ego. The sum of the conscious activities associated with managing the work of an organization.

Chronos. From the Greek, meaning time as a quantity. Linear, clock-measured, human-created time. The time of commerce, science, politics, and efficiency.

collective unconscious. A dimension of the unconscious psyche that is of an a priori, general, human character. It generates concepts and autonomous image symbols known as archetypes. This image-producing stratum of the psyche is also manifested in emotions and instincts. Synonymous with objective psyche.

complex. A cluster of unconscious contents with an archetype at its core, which is part of the subjective unconscious or organization unconscious.

conscious(ness). Under control of the ego or of an organization's center of consciousness.

constellation/constellate. The process by which an archetype becomes fixed in the subjective unconscious or organization unconscious in the form of a complex.

countertransference. The projection of the analyst's complexes onto the client or the consultant's complexes onto the client organization.

depth psychology. A group of psychological theories and associated practices that deal with unconscious processes and structures. The psychologies of Jung, Freud, and Assagioli are examples.

Eclectic Psychodynamic Organization Theory. A set of ideas about organizational dynamics grounded in organizational culture theory, the symbolic culture model, and organizational psychodynamics. This school draws with equal comfort on Rank, Assagioli, Freud, Jung, and others in creating frameworks for explaining unconscious motivation, symbolism, and meaning in organizational life.

ego. The center of individual consciousness, the point of reference for an individual's conscious experience.

ego-Self axis. The energy pathway between the conscious parts of the psyche and the unconscious parts.

extraversion. The tendency of individuals or organizations to draw energy from the outside world of people, activities, or things.

false masculine. The one-sided view of the masculine principle that recognizes only the macho, competitive, hard-edged qualities. This view fails to understand that the true masculine also has nurturing, caring, and sensitive energies.

feeling. The tendency of individuals or organizations to think and decide based on a-causal logic, subjective criteria, and the feelings and emotions of the people involved.

feminine/feminine principle. A set of psychological qualities, including soft, yielding, rounded, concave, chthonic, and yinlike. Suggestive of a "both/and" orientation to the world. Both men and women are born with this principle coded in some measure into their DNA.

function. The four mental processes Jung associated with ego consciousness: sensation, intuition, thinking, and feeling. See psychological types.

Future Search. A whole-organization change technique created by Marvin Weisbord. In a retreat setting, key members of an organization and key external stakeholders systematically examine the organization's past and present to unlock keys for the future.

generativity. The process of converting libido into original thoughts and actions.

identity. The state in which the ego or the organizational center of consciousness sees itself as being the same as something else; in Jungian psychology this something else is usually a complex. For practical purposes the state of identity is synonymous with unconsciousness.

individuation. The process by which an individual moves toward psychological wholeness.

introversion. The tendency of individuals or organizations to draw energy from the inner world of ideas, emotions, and impressions.

intuition. The tendency of individuals or organizations to take in information through a sixth sense.

Judging. The tendency of individuals or organizations to operate in a planned and organized manner.

Jungian Organization Theory. The application of analytical psychology to the understanding and changing of organizational dynamics.

Kairos. From the Greek, meaning time as a qualitative thing. The time of seasons and cycles. Its rules are those of creativity and generativity.

mandala. From the Sanskrit. A Hindu or Buddhist symbol, usually a circle enclosing a square. Reputed to have magical healing powers. Seen by Jung as a symbol of the archetypal Self.

masculine/masculine principle. A set of psychological qualities, including hard, thrusting, angular, convex, domineering, and yang-like. Suggestive of an "either/or" orientation to the world. Both women and men are born with this principle coded in some measure into their DNA.

Myers-Briggs type theory. The theory of psychological types developed by Katherine Briggs and Isabel Briggs Myers based on Jung's concept of typology with the addition of the dimensions of Judging and Perceiving attitudes.

objective psyche. See collective unconscious.

Open Space Technology. A whole-organization change technique created by Harrision Owen. In a retreat setting, members of an organization come together with no preconceived agenda to grapple with a major organizational issue. The proceedings are fluid and highly democratic.

organization development (OD). A set of theories and techniques for bringing about managed organizational change. Based largely on the values of humanistic psychology and the work of social psychologist Kurt Lewin.

organization unconscious. The set of psychological dynamics and contents unique to a particular organization that is beyond the conscious control of those who manage and lead the organization.

organizational assessment. The diagnosis of an organization's problems and potentials carried out from a Jungian perspective.

organizational psyche. The whole of an organization's psychodynamic activity, conscious and unconscious. Also, the organization's soul.

organizational transformation. Organizational transformation is an emerging set of behavioral science theories and techniques that is on the cutting edge of planned change. It has been called second generation organization development. Connected to transpersonal psychology, organizational transformation seeks to harness the full range of human potential—conscious and unconscious—to the fundamental reorienting of organizational life.

organizational whole-making. The processes and interventions an organization undergoes as it consciously sets out to engage its unconscious parts.

organizational wholeness. Roughly analogous to individuated wholeness for an individual. The state of completeness in which an organization lives out a full and unique expression of the Archetype of Organization.

participation mystique. A state of unconscious psychological identity with another person or entity. Also referred to as projective identification.

patriarchy. Governance by men and women who have forsaken their feminine principles. See false masculine.

Perceiving. The tendency of individuals or organizations to operate in spontaneous and flexible ways.

persona. From the Latin word for *mask*. The aspect of the personality that one presents to the outside world. It expresses all dimensions of the psyche and is therefore only partly conscious.

personal (subjective) unconscious. The part of the psyche that is not controlled by the ego and which is distinct from the collective unconscious. Its contents include repressed material and the complexes.

projection. The process of externalizing or objectifying what is primarily subjective and usually unconscious.

psyche. The psychological totality of the individual. The composite of all human non-somatic capacities, both conscious and unconscious.

Psychoanalytic Organization Theory. The application of psychoanalytical tools and concepts to the analysis of organizational psychodynamics. Scholars in this school would probably argue that, while there is unconscious life in organizations, there is no organization unconscious.

psychological types. A part of Jung's theory of the psyche which hypothesizes that an individual's ego has one of two characteristic orientations toward each of the following: energy (extraversion or introversion), data (sensation or intuition), and decision making (thinking or feeling). See function and attitude.

public face. The rough analogy in the organizational psyche for the persona. A system of energy on the psychological boundary between the organization and its environment.

polarity. Jung believed that there must always be psychological poles, so that the equilibrating process, which is psychic energy, can take place.

Self. The center of the individual personality. The archetype of psychological wholeness.

sensation. The tendency of individuals or organizations to take in information through the five senses and to notice what is actual.

shadow. That part of the subjective unconscious that is repressed as the ego forms.

Sociodynamic Culture Theory. A subset of organizational culture theory that uses the tools of social psychology to analyze the symbolic—and sometimes unconscious—side of organizational life.

symbol. Comes from the Greek *symbolon,* meaning *token of identity*. It connotes the putting together of two halves to create a whole. A symbol is the outward manifestation of an archetype.

temenos. Greek for container. In Jungian analysis this is the concept of the safe place where the exploration of the psyche can take place.

thinking. The tendency of individuals or organizations to think and decide based on causal logic and objective criteria.

transcendent function. The uniting symbol. The process whereby the individual psyche or organizational psyche—often in a dream—yields the solution to a psychological dilemma, a struggle between consciousness and the unconscious.

transference. The process in which the client organization transfers to the consultant (or the client to the analyst) feelings that were generated by experience with a past figure or feelings that arise out of archetypal contents.

Transpersonal Psychology. Most closely associated with Roberto Assagioli—deals with the unconscious connections between the individual, the collective unconscious, and all of creation. Some see Jung as the spiritual "father" of this tradition. The school has strong links to humanistic psychology (May, Perls, Rogers, and Maslow).

typology. See psychological types.

unconscious. Not controlled by the individual's ego or the organization's center of consciousness.

wholeness. Psychological completeness. The goal of the individuation process for the individual and of the whole-making process for the organization.

RE | SOURCES

John Corlett, Ph.D.
corlettj@mindspring.com

Carol S. Pearson, Ph.D.
Center for Archetypal Studies and Applications (CASA)
P.O. Box 73
College Park, MD 20741-0073
301-277-8042
Fax: 301-864-2977
www.herowithin.com

Center for Applications of Psychological Type, Inc.
2815 NW 13th Street
Gainesville FL 32641
800-777-2278 (toll-free USA only)
352-375-0160
www.capt.org

For more information about related publications or to purchase the *Organizational and Team Culture Indicator*™ for Individuals* or *Organizational and Team Culture Indicator*™ for Organizations†, the *Pearson-Marr Archetype Indicator*™, or the *Myers-Briggs Type Indicator*® † instruments, please contact Center for Applications of Psychological Type, Inc.

* *The OTCI for Individuals and the PMAI instruments are unrestricted and are available for purchase from the Center for Applications of Psychological Type, Inc.*

† *Please note that the OTCI for Organizations and the MBTI instruments are restricted and may only be administered by qualified practitioners. Contact CAPT or visit the website for more information about contacting a qualified practitioner or about becoming qualified to administer either of these assessment tools.*

REFER | ENCES

Abt, Theodor. *Progress Without Loss of Soul*. Wilmette IL: Chiron Publications, 1988.

Alevesson, Mats. On the Popularity of Organizational Culture in *Acta Sociologica*, Vol. 33, No. 1, 1990.

Allen, Robert F., Judd Allen, Charlotte Kraft, and Barry Certner. *The Organizational Unconscious*. Morristown NJ: Human Resources Institute, 1987.

Allen, Robert F., and Frank Dyer. A Tool for Tapping the Organizational Unconscious in *Personnel Journal*, March, 1980.

Allport, Floyd H. *Institutional Behavior*. New York NY: Greenwood Press, 1933.

Argyris, Chris. *Integrating the Individual and the Organization*. New York NY: Wiley, 1964.

Assagioli, Roberto. *Psychosynthesis*. London, England: Penguin Books, 1965.

Assagioli, Roberto. *The Act of Will*. New York NY: Viking Press, 1973.

Barry, David. Making the Invisible Visible: Using Analogically-based Methods to Surface Unconscious Organizational Processes in *Organization Development Journal*, Vol. 12, No. 4, Winter, 1994.

Beebe, John. Psychological Types in Transference, Countertransference, and Therapeutic Interaction, in *Chiron: A Review of Jungian Analysis*, 1984.

Beebe, John. *Integrity in Depth*. College Station TX: Texas A&M University Press, 1992.

Bion, Wilfred R. Group Dynamics, A Re-view in *The International Journal of Psycho-analysis*, No. 33, 1952.

Bion, Wilfred R. *Experiences in Groups*. London, England: Tavistock Publications, 1961.

Bohm, David, and F. David Peat. *Science, Order and Creativity: A Dramatic New Look at the Creative Roots of Science and Life*. New York NY: Bantam Books, 1987.

Bolen, Jean Shinoda. *Goddesses in Everywoman*. New York NY: Harper and Row, 1984.

Bolen, Jean Shinoda. *Gods in Everyman*. New York NY: Harper and Row, 1989.

Bridges, William. *The Character of Organizations: Using Jungian Type in Organization Development*. Palo Alto CA: CPP, 1992.

Briggs, John, and F. David Peat. *Turbulent Mirror*. New York NY: Harper and Row, 1989.

Capra, Fritjof. *The Turning Point*. New York NY: Simon and Schuster, 1982.

Colman, Arthur D. *Up From Scapegoating: Awakening Consciousness in Groups*. Wilmette IL: Chiron Publications, 1995.

Colman, Arthur D., and W. Harold Bexton, eds. *Group Relations Reader 1.* Washington, DC: A. K. Rice Institute, 1975.

Collins, James C., and Jerry I. Porras. *Built To Last.* New York NY: HarperBusiness, 1994.

Conforti, Michael. *Field, Form, and Fate: Patterns in Mind, Nature, and Psyche.* Woodstock CT: Spring Publications, Inc., 1999.

Corlett, Eleanor S., and Nancy B. Millner. *Navigating Mid-life Using Typology as a Guide.* Palo Alto CA: CPP, 1993.

Corlett, John G. The Organization as Psyche: A Jungian Cartography of Organizational Psychodynamics in *Harvest—Journal for Jungian Studies,* Vol. 42, No. 2, 1996.

Corlett, John G. Another Look at Chin and Benne: Is There a Fourth Strategy for Effecting Change? in *OD Practitioner,* Vol. 32, No. 3, 2000.

Cusumano, Michael A., and Richard W. Selby. *Microsoft Secrets.* New York NY: The Free Press, 1995.

DeBoard, Robert. *The Psychoanalysis of Organizations.* London, England: Tavistock, 1978.

Denhardt, Robert B. *In the Shadow of the Organization.* Lawrence KS: University of Kansas Press, 1981.

Denison, Daniel R., and Aneil K. Mishra. Toward a Theory of Organizational Culture and Effectiveness in *Organizational Science,* Vol. 6, No. 2, March–April, 1995.

Diamond, Michael. *The Unconscious Life of Organizations.* Westport CT: Quorum Books, 1993.

Edinger, Edward F. *Ego and Archetype.* New York NY: Penguin Books, 1972.

Fincher, Susanne F. *Creating Mandalas.* Boston MA: Shambhala, 1991.

Fox, Matthew. *The Reinvention of Work.* San Francisco CA: Harper Collins Publishers, 1994.

Freud, Sigmund (J. Strachey, ed. and trans.). *New Introductory Lectures on Psychoanalysis.* London, England: Hogarth Press, 1964.

Freud, Sigmund (J. Strachey, ed. and trans.). *An Outline of Psychoanalysis.* London, England: Hogarth Press, 1964.

Frost, Peter J., et al. *Organizational Culture.* Beverly Hills CA: Sage, 1985.

Goodwin, B. C. *Theoretical Biology: Epigenetic and Evolutionary Order from Complex Systems.* Baltimore MD: Johns Hopkins University Press, 1989.

Gordon, R. Reflections on Curing and Healing, in *Analytical Psychology,* Vol. 24, No. 3, 1979.

Graves, Robert. *The Greek Myths.* Baltimore MD: Penguin Books, 1955.

Grof, Stanislav. *Beyond the Brain: Birth, Death and Transcendence in Psychotherapy.* Albany NY: SUNY Press, 1985.

Grof, Stanislav. *The Adventure of Self-Discovery.* Albany NY: SUNY Press, 1988.

Hall, C. S. *A Primer of Freudian Psychology.* New York NY: World, 1954.

Handy, Charles. *Gods of Management*. London, England: Souvenir Press, 1978.

Hardy, Jean. *A Psychology with a Soul*. London, England: Routledge and Kegan Paul, 1987.

Heron, John. *Feeling and Personhood: Psychology in Another Key*. London, England: Sage, 1992.

Hillman, James. *A Blue Fire: Selected Writings*. New York NY: HarperCollins, 1989.

Hillman, James, and Michael Ventura. *We've Had a Hundred Years of Psychotherapy and the World's Getting Worse*. New York NY: HarperCollins, 1992.

Hirschhorn, Larry. *The Workplace Within*. Cambridge MA: MIT Press, 1990.

Hirsh, Sandra K. *Using the Myers-Briggs Type Indicator in Organizations*. Palo Alto CA: CPP. 1985.

Hirsh, Sandra K., and Jean M. Kummerow. *Introduction to Type in Organizations*. Palo Alto CA: CPP, 1990.

Illing, H. A. C. G. Jung on the Present Trend in Group Psychotherapy in *Human Relations,* Vol. 10, 1957.

Jacobi, Jolande. *Complex/Archetype/Symbol in the Psychology of C.G. Jung*. Princeton NJ: Princeton University Press, 1959.

Jacobi, Jolande. *The Way of Individuation*. New York NY: New American Library, 1965.

Jantsch, Erich. *Design For Evolution*. New York NY: Braziller, 1975.

Johnson, Robert A. *He: Understanding Male Psychology*. New York NY: Harper and Row, 1974.

Johnson, Robert A. *She: Understanding Feminine Psychology*. New York NY: Harper and Row, 1976.

Johnson, Robert A. Lecture at Journey into Wholeness Conference. Hendersonville NC, 1989.

Johnson, Robert A. Lecture at Journey into Wholeness Conference. Hendersonville NC, 1999.

Jung, C. G. *Psychological Types (Collected Works 6)*. Princeton NJ: Princeton University Press 1921 (1971).

Jung, C. G. *On the Nature of the Psyche (from Collected Works 8)*. Princeton NJ: Princeton University Press, 1928/1946 (1960).

Jung, C. G. *Modern Man in Search of a Soul*. San Diego CA: Harvest Books, 1933.

Jung, C. G. *Two Essays on Analytical Psychology (Collected Works 7)*. Princeton NJ: Princeton University Press, 1935/1943 (1953).

Jung, C. G. The Spirit Mercurius in *Collected Works 13*. Princeton NJ: Princeton University Press, 1948.

Jung, C. G. Synchronicity in *Collected Works 8*. Princeton NJ: Princeton University Press, 1952 (1960).

Jung, C. G. *Symbols of Transformation (Collected Works 5)*. Princeton NJ: Princeton University Press, 1952 (1956).

Jung, C. G. *The Development of Personality (Collected Works, 17)*. Princeton NJ: Princeton University Press, 1954.

Jung, C. G. *The Practice of Psychotherapy (Collected Works 16)*. Princeton NJ: Princeton University Press, 1954.

Jung, C. G. *The Undiscovered Self*. New York NY: New American Library, 1957.

Jung, C. G. *The Archetypes and the Collective Unconscious (Collected Works 9, Part I)*. Princeton NJ: Princeton University Press, 1959.

Jung, C. G. *Aion: Research into the Phenomenology of the Self (Collected Works 9, Part II)*. Princeton NJ: Princeton University Press, 1959.

Jung, C. G. *Civilization in Transition (Collected Works, 10)*. Princeton NJ: Princeton University Press, 1964.

Jung, C. G. *Memories, Dreams, and Reflections*. New York NY: Vintage Books, 1965.

Jung, C. G. The Stages of Life in Joseph Campbell, ed., *The Portable Jung*. New York NY: Viking, 1971.

Jung, C. G. *Dreams*. Princeton NJ: Princeton University Press, 1974.

Jung, C. G. *Aspects of the Masculine*. Princeton NJ: Princeton University Press, 1989.

Kast, Verena. *The Dynamics of Symbols*. New York NY: Fromm International Publishing Corporation, 1992.

Kerenyi, C. *The Gods of the Greeks*. New York NY: Thames and Hudson, Inc., 1951 (1988).

Kets de Vries, M. F. R., and D. Miller. *The Neurotic Organization*. San Francisco CA: Jossey-Bass, 1984.

Keirsey, David, and Marilyn Bates. *Please Understand* Me. Del Mar CA: Prometheus Nemesis Book Company, 1984.

Krefting, Linda, and Peter J. Frost. Untangling Webs, Surfing Waves, and Wildcatting in Frost et al., eds., *Organizational Culture*. Beverly Hills CA: Sage, 1985.

Kroeger, Otto, with Janet Thuesen. *Type Talk at Work*. New York NY: Delacorte Press, 1992.

Laszlo, Ervin. *Introduction to Systems Philosophy*. New York NY: Gordon and Breach, 1972.

Levine, David, ed. *The Fables of Aesop*. Boston MA: Gambit Publishing, 1975.

Levy, Amir, and Uri Merry. *Organizational Transformation: Approaches, Strategies, Theories*. New York NY: Praeger, 1986.

Manes, Stephen, and Paul Andrews. *Gates: How Microsoft's Mogul Reinvented An Industry—And Made Himself the Richest Man in America*. New York NY: Doubleday, 1993.

Mark, Margaret, and Carol S. Pearson. *The Hero and The Outlaw: Building Extraordinary Brands Through the Power of Archetypes*. New York NY: McGraw Hill, 2001.

Marshak, Robert J., and Judith H. Katz. Covert Processes and Revolutionary Change in M. McDonald, ed., *Forging Revolutionary Partnerships: Organization Development Network Conference Proceedings*. Portland OR: Organization Development Network, 1990.

Marshak, Robert J., and Judith H. Katz. Keys to Unlocking Covert Processes in M. McDonald, ed.,

Building: Ourselves, Our Work, Our Organizations, Our World. Portland OR: Organization Development Network, 1991a.

Marshak, Robert J., and Judith H. Katz. Covert Processes at Work in *CBODN Newsletter,* Vol. 6, No. 2, 1991b.

Marshak, Robert J., and Judith H. Katz. *The Covert Processes Workbook.* Self published, 1994.

Mattoon, Mary Ann. *Jungian Psychology in Perspective.* New York NY: The Free Press, 1981.

McWhinney, Will. Meta-Praxis: A Framework for Making Complex Changes in Allan Mohrman et al, eds., *Large-Scale Organizational Change.* San Francisco CA: Jossey-Bass, 1989.

McWhinney, Will. *Paradigms and System Theories.* Santa Barbara CA: Fielding Institute, 1991.

McWhinney, Will, and J. Batista. How Remythologizing Can Revitalize Organizations in *Organization Dynamics,* Autumn, Vol. 17, No. 3, 1988.

Menninger, Roy W. The Impact of Group Relations Conferences on Organizational Growth in *Group Relations Reader 1.* Washington, DC: A.K. Rice Institute, 1975.

Meyer, Eugene L. Pr. George's Says Pawnshops Put County's Image in Hock in *The Washington Post,* January 29, 1997.

Mindell, Arnold. *Sitting in the Fire: Large Group Transformation Using Conflict and Diversity.* Portland OR: Lao Tse Press, 1995.

Mitroff, Ian I., *Stakeholders of the Organizational Mind.* San Francisco CA: Jossey-Bass, 1984.

Mitroff, Ian I. and Robert H. Kilmann. Stories Managers Tell: A New Tool for Organizational Problem Solving in *Management Review,* July, 1975.

Moore, Robert, and Douglas Gillette. *The Magician Within: Accessing the Shaman in the Male Psyche.* New York NY: Avon Books, 1993.

Morgan, Gareth. *Images of Organization.* Newbury Park CA: Sage, 1986.

Myers, Isabel Briggs. *Gifts Differing.* Palo Alto CA: CPP, 1980.

Neumann, Erich. *The Origins and History of Consciousness.* New York NY: Pantheon, 1954.

Neumann, Erich. *The Child.* New York NY: Putnam, 1973.

Obholzer, Anton, and Zagier Roberts. *Unconscious at Work: Individual and Organizational Stress in the Human Services.* New York NY: Routledge, 1994.

Olson, Edwin E. The Transcendent Function in Organizational Change in *The Journal of Applied Behavioral Science,* Vol. 26, No. 1, 1990.

Owen, Harrison. *Open Space Technology: A User's Guide.* Potomac MD: Abbott Publishing Co, 1992.

Owen, Harrison. *The Millennium Organization.* Potomac MD: Abbott Publishing Co., 1994.

Pearson, Carol S. *The Hero Within.* San Francisco CA: Harper and Row, 1986.

Pearson, Carol S. *Awakening the Heroes Within.* San Francisco CA: Harper, 1991.

Pearson, Carol S. *Invisible Forces I.* Gladwyne PA: Type and Archetype Press, 1997.

Pearson, Carol S. *Thinking About Business Differently: Organizational Systems and Leadership Archetypes.* Aliso Viejo CA: InnoVision Communications, 1998.

Pearson, Carol S. *Organizational and Team Culture Indicator.* Gainesville FL: CAPT, in press.

Pearson, Carol S., and Hugh Marr. *Introduction to Archetypes.* Gainesville, FL: CAPT, 2002.

Pearson, Carol S., and Sharon V. Seivert. *Magic at Work.* New York NY: Currency/Doubleday, 1995.

Petzinger, Thomas, Jr. Self-organization Will Free Employees to Act Like Bosses in *Wall Street Journal,* January 3, 1997.

Pondy, Louis R., Gareth Morgan, Peter J. Frost, and Thomas C. Dandridge. *Organizational Symbolism.* Greenwich CT: JAI Press, 1983.

Presthus, Robert. *The Organizational Society.* New York NY: St. Martin's, 1978.

Quinn, Robert E. *Beyond Rational Management.* San Francisco CA: Jossey-Bass, 1988.

Quinn, Robert E., and Kim S. Cameron, eds. *Paradox and Transformation.* Cambridge MA: Ballinger Publishing Co., 1988.

Ray, Michael, and Alan Rinzler. *The New Paradigm in Business.* New York NY: Tarcher/Putnam, 1993.

Rayner, Bruce. Trial-By-Fire Transformation: An Interview with Globe Metallurgical's Arden C. Sims, in *Harvard Business Review,* May–June, 1992.

Samuels, Andrew. *Jung and the Post-Jungians.* London, England: Tavistock-Routledge, 1985.

Samuels, Andrew. *A Critical Dictionary of Jungian Analysis.* London, England: Routledge and Kegan Paul, 1986.

Schein, Edgar. *Organizational Culture and Leadership.* San Francisco CA: Jossey-Bass, 1985.

Segal, Morley. *Points of Influence.* San Francisco CA: Jossey-Bass, 1997.

Sheldrake, Rupert. *The New Science of Life: The Hypothesis of Formative Causation.* Boston MA: Houghton & Mifflin Company, 1981.

Sheldrake, Rupert. Mind, Memory and Archetype in *Psychological Perspectives.* Vol. 9, 1984.

Silverman, David. *The Theory of Organisations.* New York NY: Basic Books, 1971.

Sinclair, Amanda. Approaches to Organizational Culture and Ethics in *Journal of Business Ethics,* Vol. 12, No. 1, 1993.

Singer, June. *Boundaries of the Soul: The Practice of Jung's Psychology.* New York NY: Doubleday, 1972.

Slater, Robert. *The New GE.* Homewood IL: Business One Irwin, 1993.

Srivastva, Surest, and David L. Cooperrider. *Appreciative Management and Leadership: The Power of Positive Thought in Organizations.* San Francisco CA: Jossey-Bass, 1990.

Stein, Murray. *In Midlife.* Dallas TX: Spring Publications, 1983.

Stein, Murray. The Aims and Goals of Jungian Analysis in M. Stein, ed., *Jungian Analysis,* Boston MA: Shambhala, 1984.

Stein, Murray. *Practicing Wholeness.* New York NY: Continuum, 1996a.

Stein, Murray. Lecture at Journey Into Wholeness, Inc. Conference. Hendersonville NC, 1996b.

Stein, Murray, and John Hollwitz, eds. *Psyche at Work.* Wilmette IL: Chiron, 1992.

Stevens, Anthony. *Archetypes: A Natural History of the Self.* New York NY: Viking Penguin, 1991.

Swoboda, Frank. Talking Management with Chairman Welch in *The Washington Post,* March 23, 1997.

Thompson, William. *At the Edge of History.* New York NY: Harper and Row, 1971.

Tichy, Noel M., and Ram Charan. Speed, Simplicity, Self-Confidence: An Interview with Jack Welch in *Harvard Business Review,* September–October, 1989.

Tichy, Noel M., and Stratford Sherman. *Control Your Destiny or Someone Else Will,* New York NY: Doubleday, 1993.

Tyler, Sam. *The Excellence Files.* Cambridge MA: Enterprise Media, 1997.

Walsh, Mary Williams. Where GE Falls Short: Diversity at the Top in *New York Times,* September 3, 2000.

Weber, Max. *The Theory of Social and Economic Organisation.* New York NY: Free Press, 1964.

Weisbord, Marvin R. *Productive Workplaces.* San Francisco CA: Jossey-Bass, 1987.

Weisbord, Marvin R. *Discovering Common Ground.* San Francisco CA: Berrett-Koehler Publishers, 1992.

Wheatley, Margaret. *Leadership and the New Science: Learning About Organization from an Orderly Universe.* San Francisco CA: Berrett Koehler, 1992.

White, Joseph B. How a Creaky Factory Got Off the Hit List, Won Respect at Last in *Wall Street Journal,* December 26, 1996.

Whitmont, Edward C. *The Symbolic Quest.* Princeton NJ: Princeton University Press, 1969.

Wilber, Ken. *No Boundary: Eastern and Western Approaches to Personal Growth.* Boulder CO: Shambhala, 1979.

Wilmer, Harry A. *Practical Jung.* Wilmette IL: Chiron Publications, 1987.

Wilmer, Harry A. *Understandable Jung.* Wilmette IL: Chiron Publications, 1994.

Wink, Walter. *Unmasking the Powers.* Philadelphia PA: Fortress Press, 1986.

Working Woman. Women, Power, and the New GE. December, 1992.

Zuckerman, M. R., and L. J. Hatala. *Incredibly American: Releasing The Heart of Quality.* Milwaukee WI: ASQC Quality Press, 1992.

IN|DEX

active imagination 62, 96, 104, 183

addiction 100

Aesop 1, 2, 194

affirmative action 110

alchemical 22, 102, 113

alchemy 11

amazon 26

analogically mediated inquiry 63

analytical Psychology xi–xiii, 13, 110, 183, 192

anima xi, 30, 183

animus xi, 30, 183

Archetypal Leadership Styles Survey xvi, 59, 88, 139, 142, 169

archetypal psychology xiv, 110, 183

archetypal Self xi, xii, 8, 13, 18, 26, 95, 104, 139, 141, 151, 155, 183

Archetype of Organization 13–24, 29, 30, 40, 41–50, 53–65, 73, 76, 78, 79, 83, 86, 89, 90, 92–97, 101, 109, 111, 119–121, 126, 143, 168, 183

Archetypes of Family Culture xvi, 179

art (as method of intervention) 62, 63

as if xiv, 2, 11, 46–48, 53, 56, 60, 75, 102, 104

attitude
    psychological type 183
    relating to center of consciousness 39, 96, 126
    relating to ego 32

authenticity (of leader) 86

authoritarian management 24

balancing (of energy) 8, 23, 37, 50, 55, 65, 72

Baltimore Orioles 96

bipolarity (regarding energy) 8

Bohm, David 112

boundary 128, 130, 131, 181

boundary (of organizational psyche) 19, 38, 56, 103, 126, 128, 130–131

brainstorming 64

brand 22. *See also* public face
    identity 22, 32, 34, 56, 76–77, 81, 123, 126, 130

branding 34, 56, 75, 77, 100

Bridges, William 31

butterfly xii

Camelot 64

Caregiver 17, 19, 21, 33–34, 46, 73–74, 76

Caregiver complex 17, 121, 144

Cartesian 108

catalyst 85, 101, 152

center of consciousness 27–34, 38–41, 53–54, 71, 83, 85, 88–89, 95, 99–100, 103, 107, 109, 122, 126, 127, 128, 130, 142, 152, 184. *See also* organizational ego

change xvi, 9, 21, 29, 46, 54, 59–65, 71, 75–76, 79, 83, 92, 96–97, 100–101, 103, 110–111, 127, 152, 185, 186

change efforts xvi, 100

chaos theory 112

chronos 54, 61, 184

Coca Cola 39, 56

codependency 21

collage 63

collective unconscious xii, xiv, 7, 13–15, 17, 19, 38, 43–44, 46, 48, 53–56, 61–66, 83, 86, 89, 95, 104, 108, 126–128, 130–131, 183–184, 186–187. *See also* objective unconscious

command and control 82

competitiveness 90, 96

completeness. *See* wholeness

complex. *See* organizational complex

compulsiveness 46

Conforti, Michael 112

congruence (as characteristic of consultant) ix

conscious xi, 2, 7–11, 13–16, 19, 24, 27–29, 32, 34, 44, 46, 49, 54–56, 61–62, 64–65, 71, 77, 87, 91, 94, 97, 99, 101, 104, 109–110, 122–123, 126, 130, 139, 151, 184

consciousness 8–13, 16, 27–34, 37–48, 50, 53, 54–66, 71–72, 74, 83, 85, 88, 89, 90, 95, 96-97, 100–103, 107–111, 122–123, 126–128, 130–131, 142, 152, 184

consensual 20

consensus 20, 109

constellate(ed) 17, 19, 23, 60, 65, 73, 78, 183, 184

constellating 17, 86

constellation 184

container (for psychological work) 14, 19, 54, 101, 103, 111, 152, 187

control 15, 27–28, 44, 49, 56, 62, 66, 78, 89, 92

control complex 47

cosmology 113

countertransference 102–103, 184

creative fantasy (as means of intervention) 62

creative tension 93, 168

creativity xiv, 10, 16, 21, 37, 44, 46, 54, 109

Creator 19, 21, 33, 78

culture. *See* organizational culture

decision making 28–29, 31, 41–42, 61, 78, 85

Defense Personnel Support Center 61

democratic 28, 82, 185

demonic (energy of archetype) 19, 46, 47

denial xi, 2, 8, 38, 41, 45–46, 50, 59, 74, 76, 100, 127

dependent 103, 109

depth psychology 2, 184

DeVito, Danny 111

dialectical 9

dialogue 37, 44, 55, 57, 62, 86, 97, 100–101, 109–110, 130, 183

differentiation 43, 54, 90

diversity 40, 43, 59, 86, 108–110

diversity panels 59

drama (as means of intervention) 62

drawing (as means of intervention) 63

dream(s) 64, 77, 87, 95–96, 104, 122, 127, 138–139, 150–151, 187

dualistic thinking 20

dynamic homeostasis 10

dysfunction (of an organization) 48, 62, 92

Eclectic Psychodynamic Organization Theory xiv, 184

ego xi, 8, 16, 29, 31, 43, 49, 86, 88, 95, 105, 122, 139, 141, 151, 154, 184

   ego consciousness 185

   ego-centric 89

   ego-directed 27, 48, 54

   ego-Self axis 184

emotion 18, 39, 45–46, 88, 100, 105, 119, 168, 184

emotional intelligence 56

employee involvement 28, 82

energy. *See* psychic energy

entropy 112, 113

environment (of the organization) 7, 18–19, 24, 32–34, 38, 41–43, 47, 56, 65–66, 75, 90, 92, 94, 97, 109, 123, 187

Equal Employment Opportunity 110

equilibrating (as an energy process) 187

eros 113

ethics 29, 99

Explorer 19, 21–22, 33, 76

Extraversion/extraversion 31, 123, 184, 186

false masculine 107, 184

family dysfunction 81

family unconscious 15

family-owned businesses 79

fantasy(ies) 64, 87

Feeling/feeling 16, 31–32, 45, 57, 123, 184

feminine 19, 22, 30–31, 37, 83, 108–109, 111, 122–123, 139, 151, 183–184

feminine principle 16, 45, 108, 184

Ford Motor Company 28

four-fold nature 25

Freud xi, 184

Freudian xii

Friedman, Milton 111

function 16, 185, 186

   of center of consciousness 46, 62, 64

   psychological type 16, 31–32, 45, 79, 89, 94, 101, 122, 138–139, 150–151

Future Search 60, 185

Gates, Bill 43

Gen X 82

General Electric (GE) 16, 39, 42, 46–47, 49, 58–59

generativity 46, 54, 65, 185

Globe Metallurgical, Inc. 28

goals (of organization) xiv, 2, 9, 10, 18, 22, 187

Goodwin, Brian 112

guided fantasy (as change intervention) 64

habits of mind 91

healing 30, 54, 103, 105, 106, 152, 185

heart (of an organization) xi, xiv, 18–19

Hermes 110

hermetic transformation 110–111

Hero 16, 19, 20, 22–23, 33, 47, 67, 76–77, 80–83, 121, 144

heuristic 100

Hillman, James xiii

holistic 54, 108

human capital 92, 168
human community 90–92, 139,
    142, 145
human will 9, 90
humor 15, 20

idealism 75–77, 92
identity (relating to a complex)
    22, 25, 46, 78, 86, 185
illusion of control 47
imaginal space 105
individual psyche 143, 150
individuality xii
individuation xii–xiii, 89, 99, 102,
    105, 113, 185, 187
inferior function 79, 138, 150
inflation (relating to a complex)
    46–47, 104, 106
inner work 86, 104, 139, 151,
    153
Innocent 19, 21, 33, 39, 42, 46,
    67, 76, 121, 144
innovate 66
instinct 79
integration 25, 30, 90–91, 93,
    113
integrity ix, xiv, 34, 99, 104, 105
intervention 29, 49, 59, 69
Introversion/introversion 31, 123,
    185, 186
Intuition/intuition 31, 123
intuitive energies 63
irrational xiv, xvi, 2, 49, 61
irrationality 15
ivory tower 47

Jantsch, Erich 90, 112
Jester 19, 20, 22, 33, 67, 121,
    144
Johnson & Johnson 34
Judging 31, 32, 123, 185
Jung, C. G. xi–xvi, 7–9, 13–18,
    24–27, 30–32, 35, 54, 89–90,

95–96, 100, 103–105, 110,
    112, 183–187
Jungian xi–xvi, 9, 11, 19, 27, 41,
    65, 66, 69, 89, 90, 100–104,
    106, 112, 113, 134, 146, 153,
    156
Jungian Organization Theory xi,
    xii–xvi, 24, 34, 50, 66, 84, 97,
    106, 110, 113, 185

Kairos 54, 61, 185
Kelleher, Herb 22
king 26
King Midas 66

Laszlo, Ervin 90, 112
Learning energies 22, 23
learning organization 29
learning subsystem 90–92, 139,
    143, 145, 152
libido 2, 8, 26, 47, 185
life span (of an organization) 8
life stage (of organization) 43,
    126
litmus test of love (relating to
    consultant's values) 103–104
logic 32, 45, 89, 108, 184, 187
love 22, 91, 103, 104, 152
Lover 19, 20–22, 33, 42, 67

Mae-Wan Ho 112
magic circle 64, 92, 96, 181
Magician 19, 20, 33, 67, 80–81
managed health organizations 40
managerial leader xvi, 168
mandala 19, 22, 25, 63, 64, 92,
    96–97, 139, 151, 185
map xvi, 24, 34, 50, 66, 69, 84,
    143, 153
mapping xv, 24, 34, 50, 60, 66,
    84, 95, 97, 99, 106, 150
Marx Brothers 11
masculine 16, 19, 22, 26, 30–31,

37, 40, 58, 83, 109, 111, 113,
    122–123, 139, 151, 183, 185
masculine principle 184, 185
material subsystem 90–92, 143,
    145
MBTI. See Myers-Briggs Type
    Indicator instrument
MBTI type descriptions 159
Mead, Margaret 111
meaning xii, xiv, 18–19, 22, 25,
    30, 39, 81, 86, 91, 93–94,
    104–105, 110, 112–113, 142
medicine wheel 92, 97
melancholic 26
men 30, 80, 82, 107, 184, 185,
    186
Menninger clinic 28
mergers and acquisitions 23, 48
metaphor(s) xii, 2, 92
metaphoric 87
Microsoft 43–44, 57
midlife (of organization) 44
Millennium Generation 82
mission 2, 23, 26, 29–30, 44, 49,
    75–76, 79, 86, 90–91, 105
morale 3, 10–11, 22, 37, 44, 56,
    70, 105
mores 16
Mt. Vernon College 42
Myers, Isabel 31, 185
Myers-Briggs Type Indicator
    instrument xi, xvi, 78, 86, 89,
    100, 122, 138–139, 150–151,
    159, 189
Myers-Briggs type theory xiii, 185
mysterium coniunctionis 110
myth 17, 42, 60–62, 67
mythmaker 94
mythological 14

Native American 88
navel-gazing 66
neurotic 2, 66

Newtonian 108, 113
Nike 33, 47
nonprofit 79, 105
numinous 25, 86, 104
nurturing mother 17

objective psyche 184, 185
Olson, Edwin 95, 96
Open Space Technology 49, 60, 65, 185
open system 7
opposites (as psychological phenomena) 8, 19, 62, 64, 90, 95, 96–97, 103, 110–111
organization
development xiv, xv, 66, 100, 185
shadow 15–16, 29, 33, 38, 44–46, 58–59, 89, 108, 118
unconscious 9–25, 30, 33–34, 40, 43–44, 50, 53–55, 62–63, 66, 89, 95, 99, 103, 108–110, 184, 186
organizational
angel 25
assessment xvi, 186
character 31
complex 17–18, 25, 38, 46–47, 56, 60, 76, 119, 126, 128, 130–131
culture xi, xv, 15, 23, 25–26, 34, 48, 82, 108
dynamics 9, 41, 94, 113
ego 16, 88
projection 38–39, 50, 56–57
psyche xi, xii, xiii, xiv, 7–11, 13–15, 25, 27–28, 32–34, 37–38, 41, 43, 45, 53–55, 58, 62, 66, 71, 79, 81–90, 95, 97, 101, 105, 106, 109–110, 113, 186
psychology 13, 199
science xiv
self 25

society xii
story 93
system x, 25, 29, 31, 62, 90, 101, 109, 112–113
transformation xiv, 186
whole-making 53, 54, 65, 101, 103, 105, 153, 186
wholeness 23–24, 50, 65–66, 69, 85–86, 88–89, 95, 97, 99, 104, 110–111, 186
Organizational and Team Culture Indicator instrument xi, 60, 62, 67, 72, 75–76, 80–81, 100, 117–118, 120, 123, 189
OTCI. See *Organizational and Team Culture Indicator* instrument
Other People's Money 111

paradigm 20, 79, 80, 81, 108
paradox 18–19, 23, 65, 90, 103, 106
participation mystique xi, 16, 25, 119, 186
participative management 28, 82
partnership model 100
pathological 24
pathways (toward organizational wholeness) 54–55, 130–131
patriarchal 107–108
patriarchy 108–109, 186
Pearson xv, xvii, 26, 51, 56, 67, 189
Pearson-Marr Archetype Indicator instrument iv, xi, xvi, 86, 138, 150, 189
Peat, F. David 112
Peck, Gregory 111
People energies 22
People Express 42, 59
people of color 40, 60, 108
Perceiving 31–32, 123, 185–186
persona xi, 8, 32–33, 104, 140–141, 152, 154, 186

personal unconscious 13, 24, 25, 104. *See also* subjective unconscious
phlegmatic 26
play (as an intervention) xii
PMAI. See Pearson-Marr Archetype Indicator instrument
pogo dictum 57
polar opposite 9, 19, 64, 90
polarity 11, 63–65, 111, 187
polarization 10
pole (relating to psychic energy) 94, 103, 109, 187
Post-Jungians 14
Pratt & Whitney 58
Presthus, Robert xii
processes of creative formulation 61, 106, 131
processes of understanding 55–56, 106, 130
production subsystem 90–92, 139, 143, 145, 152
projecting 179
projection xi, 8, 11, 16, 25, 38, 39–40, 46–47, 50, 55–58, 65, 74, 87, 101, 127, 130, 184, 186
psyche xi–xvi, 7,–12, 15–16, 26, 30, 35, 49, 87, 90, 96, 99, 105, 112, 141, 186
consultant's psyche 153–154
individual psyche 8, 12, 14, 17, 18, 19, 23, 51, 95, 112, 153
leader's psyche 140–141, 144–145
psychic energy 8, 11, 14, 17, 25–27, 37, 44, 47, 90.
Psychoanalytic Organization Theory xiv, 186
psychodynamic(s) xi, xii, xv, 15, 18–19, 22, 25, 43, 48, 55–56, 65, 104, 110
psychological field 15

psychological types xi, xiii, 78–79, 89, 185, 186. See also *Myers-Briggs Type Indictor* instrument
psychological wholeness xi, 8, 185, 187. *See also* wholeness
psychopomp 99
psychosis 66
psychotherapy 104
public face 32–34, 38–39, 55–57, 66, 71–72, 76, 81, 123, 127, 130. *See also* persona

quantum theory 112
quaternity 26
queen 26

racial memory 14
racism 15, 45–46, 59, 74, 86
rational 27, 71
rationality 45, 48, 89, 181
re-member xv, 89, 113
re-membering 53
readiness (of an organization for change) 99
rebalancing (of psychic energy) 8, 37, 65, 83
reification xiv, xvii
renewal 26, 45, 107, 131
repression xi, xiii, 8, 38, 40–41, 45, 59, 74, 108, 127
Results energies 22
Revolutionary 19–20, 33, 56, 67, 80–81
royal marriage 111, 113
Ruler 19, 21–22, 33, 47, 61, 63, 67, 71–72, 76, 78–80

sacred stories 76
Sage 17, 19, 21, 33, 47, 67, 71–72, 76, 80–81
sanguine 26
scapegoating 20, 45, 58, 101

scientific management 45, 48, 89
Self/self. See archetypal Self
self-destructive 9
Self-organization 29, 30
self-organizing 131
self-regulating 10, 112
self-renewal 7, 26
Sensing/sensation 16, 31, 57, 123, 185–187
shadow xi, 2, 8, 15–16, 23, 29, 32–34, 37–39, 44–46, 54–55, 58, 60, 65, 71, 72, 74, 79, 80, 83, 86, 88–89, 101, 104, 108, 110, 118–119, 126, 130, 138, 140, 141, 150, 152, 155, 187
shaman 26, 94
Sheldrake, Rupert 112
Sims, Arden C. 28
Sociodynamic Culture Theory xiv, 187
soul xi, xiii, 7, 49, 51, 62, 85, 86, 93, 105–106, 109–110, 142, 153
soul-searching 104
Southwest Airlines 22, 96
spirit xi, 81, 83, 94, 103, 113
spiritual 85–86, 90–93, 104–105, 139, 151
spirituality xi, xii, 75
squaring of the circle 25
Stabilizing energies 22
stage of life 23
start-up organization 30, 43
stereotyping 50
steward (referring to leader) 85–86, 90
storyteller 93
structure (of organization) 16, 18, 21, 28, 29, 32, 58, 61–62, 70, 82, 91
subjective unconscious 15, 184, 187. *See also* personal unconscious

subsystem(s) 25, 88, 90, 92–93, 142–143
symbol 2, 62–64, 92, 94–96, 103, 187
symbolic xii, 2, 63, 87, 96
symbolism 63, 184
synchronicity(ies) 8, 9, 15, 64, 65, 108
synchronistic 54, 94, 127
System Stewardship Survey xvi, 59, 83–84, 88, 139, 142, 163, 168
system thinker 7
system thinking 90

Tailhook 94
Tavistock 28
temenos ix, 103–104, 187
tension of the opposites (in organizational psychodynamics) 8, 62, 96, 97
Texas Air 42
thanatos 113
Thinking/thinking 16, 31, 35, 45, 57, 123, 187
third way (for problem solving) 15, 96
Timberland Company 111
Total Quality Management 46
trancelike 2, 112
transcendent function xi, 62, 64, 85, 95–97, 113, 143, 187
transference 102–103, 187
transformation xiv, 33, 54, 90, 97, 104, 110–13
transformative 86
transition 43, 50–51, 63, 65, 91, 96
transpersonal psychology xiv, 186–187
Trinity of Vermont 42
troubadour 101
Tylenol 34

typelike 31, 32, 57

typological 31, 45, 57, 58, 122, 127, 138, 150

Typology 31, 35, 79, 89, 185, 187. *See also* psychological types

unconscious xi, xii, xiv, xvi, 2–3, 7–12, 13–25, 27–35, 37–50, 53–54, 59, 61, 63–65, 71, 77, 83, 86–87, 94–95, 97, 99, 100–113, 118–119, 122, 126–127, 130, 142, 152, 187

unconscious dynamics xiv, 54, 104

Underwood, Paula 88

United Parcel Service 31

uniting symbol 187

vision 2, 29, 42–43, 63, 74, 77, 81, 92, 94, 142

visioning 49

Warrior 16

Welch, Jack 39, 42, 47, 49, 58

white water 2, 66

Whole Foods, Inc. 29

whole-making (process) 53–55, 58, 60–62, 65, 69, 72, 77–78, 80, 83, 85, 101–106, 134–135, 146–147, 156–157, 187. *See also* organizational whole-making

Whole-organization change technologies 60

wholeness 2, 19, 23, 25, 43, 51, 54–55, 61, 65–66, 95, 96, 103, 106, 110, 113, 187. *See also* completeness and organizational wholeness

women 16, 30, 40, 58, 60, 80–82, 107–108, 184–186

Work-Out intervention 59

wounded healer 101, 103, 106

Zeitgeist 92

ABOUT | AUTHORS

John G. Corlett, Ph.D., is an independent organizational consultant, university lecturer, and writer. He has fifteen years of experience consulting with client organizations in the public, private and not-for-profit sectors. He is an adjunct faculty member at the University of Virginia and The Union Institute, teaching courses in organizational psychology, change management, organization theory, organization development, organizational behavior, managerial leadership, human resource management, and consulting theory and practice. He is also an adjunct faculty member at the Federal Executive Institute. His main research interest is the development of Jungian Organization Theory, the application of C. G. Jung's psychology to the analysis of organizational change and dynamics. He has published articles on this and related topics in the *OD Practitioner* and *Harvest— Journal For Jungian Studies*. Dr. Corlett has lectured on Jungian Organization Theory at conferences sponsored by the Organization Development Network; the Association for Psychological Type; Journey Into Wholeness, Inc.; The Richmond Society for Jungian Psychology; and the Washington Society for Jungian Psychology. He is vice president of the board of directors of Journey into Wholeness, Inc.

Carol S. Pearson, Ph. D., is president of the Center for Archetypal Studies and Applications (CASA), Director of the Transformational Leadership Program at Georgetown University, a Senior Fellow at the James MacGregor Burns Academy of Leadership at the University of Maryland, and a part-time faculty member at the Saybrook Graduate School in Organizational Systems Inquiry. A pioneer in the field of applied Jungian psychology, she is the creator of archetypal systems which are widely used by psychologists, educators, executive coaches, and management consultants to develop individuals, leaders and organizations. She is the author of numerous books and instruments, including *The Hero Within: Six Archetypes We Live By* (Harper and Row, 1986, 1991. 1998); *Awakening the Heroes Within: Twelve Archetypes that Help Us Find Ourselves and Transform Our World* (HarperSanfrancisco, 1981); *Magic At Work: Camelot, Creative Leadership and Everyday Miracles* (Doubleday, 1995); *Invisible Forces: Harnessing the Power of Archetypes to Improve Your Career and Your Organization* (Type and Archetypes Press, 1997); and *The Hero and The Outlaw: Building Extraordinary Brands Through the Power of Archetypes* (McGraw-Hill 2000, co-author Margaret Mark). She is also the author of the *Pearson-Marr Archetypal Indicator™* (*PMAI™*, co-author Hugh Marr) and the *Organizational and Team Culture Indicator™* (*OTCI™*). Dr. Pearson is a former academic vice president of Goucher College, tenured faculty member at the University of Maryland, College Park, and senior editor of *The Inner Edge: a Resource for Enlightened Business Practice*. She currently trains professionals in the use of her theories, models and instrumentation and offers leadership coaching and integrative branding/organization development consulting.